Routedge Revivals

The New-Old Land of Israel

First published in 1960, *The New-Old Land of Israel* deals particularly with the excavations which have amazingly enlarged our knowledge of Bible times. The unique quality of the Bible land of Israel is that it has the thrill of a rich historic past, an ardent, bustling present and an exciting, incalculable future. It is the purpose of this book to give to the reader that thrill, to describe the historical places which have been excavated by the archaeologists and link the past with the present.

It starts with a survey of Palestine archaeology in the last hundred years, and a brief history of Jerusalem through the ages. Then it gives an account of the modern big town by the sea, Tel Aviv- Jaffa, and the ancient Roman town by the sea, Caesarea; of the Philistine city of Askalon and a biblical fortress of Judaea which are again populous: of Beersheba, the home of the patriarchs Abraham and Isaac, and now a teeming modern town which grows by thousands every year, and of a Eilat, a port of King Solomon and today of Israel to the Red Sea. This is an important read for scholars and researchers of archaeology, history of Israel, Middle East history and history in general.

The New-Old Land of Israel

Norman Bentwich

First published in 1960
by George Allen & Unwin Ltd.

This edition first published in 2024 by Routledge
4 Park Square, Milton Park, Abingdon, Oxon, OX14 4RN

and by Routledge
605 Third Avenue, New York, NY 10017

Routledge is an imprint of the Taylor & Francis Group, an informa business

© George Allen & Unwin Ltd, 1960

All rights reserved. No part of this book may be reprinted or reproduced or utilised in any form or by any electronic, mechanical, or other means, now known or hereafter invented, including photocopying and recording, or in any information storage or retrieval system, without permission in writing from the publishers.

Publisher's Note
The publisher has gone to great lengths to ensure the quality of this reprint but points out that some imperfections in the original copies may be apparent.

Disclaimer
The publisher has made every effort to trace copyright holders and welcomes correspondence from those they have been unable to contact.

A Library of Congress record exists under LCCN: 60050094

ISBN: 978-1-032-76184-8 (hbk)
ISBN: 978-1-003-47743-3 (ebk)
ISBN: 978-1-032-76185-5 (pbk)

Book DOI 10.4324/9781003477433

Second century Necropolis at Beth-Shearim Israel. Entrance to the catacombs

The New-Old Land of Israel

NORMAN BENTWICH

*Formerly Weizmann Professor of
International Relations at the
Hebrew University of Jerusalem*

Ruskin House
GEORGE ALLEN & UNWIN LTD
MUSEUM STREET · LONDON

First published in Great Britain 1960

This book is copyright under the Berne Convention. Apart from any fair dealing for the purpose of private study, research, criticism, or review, as permitted under the Copyright Act, 1956, no portion may be reproduced by any process without written permission. Enquiries should be addressed to the publisher.

© *George Allen & Unwin Ltd, 1960*

*Printed in Great Britain
in 11 on 13 Pilgrim type
by
East Midland Printing Company Limited
Bury St. Edmunds, Peterborough, Kettering
and elsewhere*

PREFACE

This book is designed to give the common reader interested in Biblical archaeology and in Israel of today an account of the exciting finds of antiquity which, in recent years, have been, and are being, made in different parts of the country, and to relate them to present developments. The peculiar attraction of the discovery of antiquity in the Land of the Bible is that it is linked with the rebirth of the Jewish Nation in its historical environment. The 'least of lands' is the most historical; and nowhere else are landscape and history so completely fused. It was a cradle of human civilization; and the neighbouring countries were the nurseries of that civilization. Here men started to cultivate the soil, first with stone, and then with metal, implements. Here he began to work the potter's wheel, here he invented alphabetic writing. The oldest walled town in the world is Jericho. Jerusalem and Jaffa, Beersheba and Askalon, have a continuous history of 4,000 years. Our knowledge of the relations between the peoples and cultures of antiquity increases every year, as the spade of the excavators, many of them amateurs, reveals, and the knowledge of the scholars illuminates, the treasures of the past. Eras of human endeavour, which were scarcely conceived in the last century, have been disclosed vividly; and the Land of Israel, more than any other field of antiquarian research, offers a picture of the continuity of civilization from its dawn. It is an open-air museum; and the archaeological activities have become the funnel through which the achievements of the past merge into the achievements of the present.

I have dealt particularly with the dramatic diggings in the land which have been carried out since the establishment of the State of Israel.

For the illustrations I am grateful to Professor Nahman Avigad of the Department of Archaeology of the Hebrew University of Jerusalem, to the Israel Government Tourist Office in London, and to Mr Schweig, the official photographer of several archaeological expeditions, for permission to reproduce photographs of places and excavations in Israel. I am beholden to Dr Kathleen Kenyon and the Palestine Exploration Fund for the use of the photograph of her excavation of the Jericho Mound, which has revealed the oldest city in history.

Part of Chapters VII-X appeared in the Contemporary Review.

NORMAN BENTWICH

CONTENTS

		page
PREFACE		7
I	The Archaeology of the Land of Israel	15
II	Jerusalem	32
III	The Coastal Plain, Jaffa and Caesarea	53
IV	The Judean Foothills. Gezer and Modiin	66
V	The Philistine Coast: Lachish and Askalon	77
VI	The Central Plain: Dor, Megiddo and Beth Shaan	89
VII	Galilee: Hazor and Beth Shearim	100
VIII	The Negev: Beersheba and Elath	115
IX	Jericho and Beth Yerah	129
X	The Dead Sea: Caves, Scrolls and Citadels	140
INDEX		158

ILLUSTRATIONS

Necropolis at Beth-Shearim		frontispiece
2	*New buildings of the Hebrew University*	facing page
	Mount Zion, overlooking the Old City	32
3	*Ossuary in Jerusalem*	33
	Third wall of Jerusalem	33
4	*An aerial view of Jaffa*	between pages
	Jaffa and Tel-Aviv	64 and 65
5	*Roman Emperor's statue*	
	Askalon, Greco-Roman statue and columns	
6	*The White Tower at Ramleh*	
7	*Model of King Solomon's stable at Megiddo*	
	Beth-Alpha. Mosaic of synagogue	
	Capital from Caesarea	
8	*Beth-Shearim: archway of the old Sanhedrin hall*	96 and 97
	Beth-Shearim: Catacomb interior	
9	*Hazor: a view of the slopes before excavation*	
	Hazor: citadel mound	
10	*Canaanite shrine found in Hazor excavation*	
11	*Timna: site of King Solomon's mines*	
	The Basilica of Byzantine Esbeita in the Negev	
12	*Beersheba: the Turkish mosque*	128 and 129
	Gulf of Akaba	
13	*One of the scrolls from the Dead Sea Cave*	
	Pottery jars in which the scrolls were found	
14	*Jericho. Looking towards the Mount of Temptation*	
15	*Potash works at Sodom*	
	Massada on the Dead Sea	

CHRONOLOGY OF THE LAND OF ISRAEL

Most of the dates are approximate

Waves of Semite Settlement	3000—2000 B.C.
Age of the Patriarchs	1900—1700
Invasion of the Hyksos	1680—1580
The Habiri invade Canaan	1480—1350
Hittite Conquest	1390—1350
Egyptian Re-Conquest	1350—1250
Israel's Exodus from Egypt	1350?
Hebrew Conquest of Canaan	1300—
Philistine Invasions	1190—1020
Kingdom of Saul, David and Solomon	1020— 926
Division of the Hebrew Kingdom	926
Israel Kings	926— 720
Judah Kings	926— 586
Siege and Fall of Jerusalem	586
Persian Rule	538— 336
Hellenistic Kingdoms	336— 168
Maccabean Rule	168— 63
Roman Rule	63 B.C.— 390 A.D.
Byzantine Empire	390— 630
Arab Conquest	630
Omayad Caliphs rule Arab Empire from Damascus	650— 750
Abbassid Caliphs rule from Bagdad	750—1000
The Seljuk Turks conquer Syria and Palestine	1070
The Crusaders capture Jerusalem and establish Latin Kingdom	1100
Saladin recaptures Jerusalem for the Moslems	1187
Mongol invasion of Palestine	1260
Crusaders expelled from Palestine	1291
Jews expelled from Spain; many take refuge in Palestine	1492
Ottoman Turks conquer the Arab Empire	1500
Napoleon Bonaparte invades Egypt and Palestine	1797—1798
British Consulate established in Jerusalem	1838
Jewish agricultural school established outside Jaffa	1870
First Jewish agricultural 'colonies' planted in Palestine	1880—1883

Theodor Herzl publishes 'The Jews' State'	1895
Turkey allied with Germany in First World War	1914
British Army captures Gaza, Jaffa, Jerusalem and Southern Palestine	1917
British Army occupy the rest of Palestine and Syria	1918
The Mandate for Palestine allotted to Great Britain	1920
Hebrew University of Jerusalem opened by Lord Balfour	1925
British Government applies to the United Nations for advice about Palestine Mandate	1947
General Assembly adopts resolution for Partition of Palestine into Jewish and Arab States	
Arabs and Jews engage in Civil War: January—May	1948
British Mandate ends May 14th	
Jews proclaim creation of State of Israel	1948
Israel admitted to the United Nations	1949

I

The Archæology of the Land of Israel

ARCHAEOLOGY is the science of antiquity; it aims at discovering and expounding the history of the human race in ancient times through the recovery of the records of the past. Those records are found in ruins and relics of ancient towns, monuments and inscriptions, vessels and jewellery, which have in part survived above the ground through the ages, and in greater part have been buried beneath the ground, and are revealed by exploration and digging. The science has been enormously developed during the last century. The new knowledge, which has been acquired in that period, about the 8,000 years of civilization before the Christian era and the first 1,000 years of that era, is as revolutionary as the new knowledge man has obtained of the physical universe by scientific experiment. Of no part of the world is that more true than of the Holy Land, the land of the Bible. Wherever you plant your foot in that land you tread on history. A hundred years ago Palestine was largely deserted and derelict. Save for Holy towns, such as Jerusalem, Jaffa, Hebron, Bethlehem, Nazareth and Tiberias, which were sacred places of Jews or Christians, and were visited through the ages by pilgrims, and save for a few biblical sites which kept their ancient name, e.g. Gaza, Askalon, Jericho, Shiloh, and for the tombs of saints, being mainly Biblical characters, visited by pilgrims, most of the places mentioned in the Bible were not identified. Little was known, too, before the middle of the 19th century, of the relations of the Hebrew people and the king-

The New Old Land of Israel

doms of Israel and Judah with the other ancient civilizations of the Orient, except what is recounted in the books of the Bible.

Following Napoleon's invasion of Egypt in 1797, French and other scholars developed a science of Egyptology, which meant, primarily, reading of the hieroglyphic inscriptions on the many temples, obelisks and tombs of the Nile valley. A great step forward was made when scholars were able to read the Greek inscription on the Rosetta Stone—found in a city of the Nile Delta—which bore also hieroglyphic writing. They discovered that the two scripts were two versions of the same story; and from that beginning they were able to get a key to picture writing, and unravel some of the mysteries of the Pharaohs and the Pyramids. A little later English and European archaeologists explored the visible monuments of the Assyrian, Babylonian and Persian kings in Mesopotamia and Persia (now called Iraq and Iran). They carried away some of the most spectacular finds to the British Museum, the Louvre in Paris, and other famous museums of antiquity. Scholars read the old language of Assyria written in picture signs, called cuneiform, by wedges on clay tablets, oven-baked, which survived in hundreds of thousands; and our knowledge of the civilization of the warlike empires, which were bound up with the history of the Holy Land, was immensely enlarged.

Scientific exploration of the Holy Land itself began in the early part of the 19th century. An American teacher of Hebrew, Edward Robinson, came to Palestine in 1838, with the purpose of identifying Bible sites. He made a great contribution to the knowledge of the topography of ancient Jerusalem. In particular, he discovered an arch near the old Temple enclosure, which he identified as a raised way spanning what was once a deep ravine between the hills of Moriah and Zion. To this day it is called Robinson's Arch. His *Physical Geography of the Holy Land* was published after his death in 1865. In that same year the Palestine Exploration Fund was founded in England, under royal patronage.

The English bible-loving people were deeply interested in the

The Archaeology of the Land of Israel

discovery of the sites of the Bible Land. And the Crimean War 1854-6, of which the immediate cause was a dispute between the Orthodox and Catholic communities about rights in the Church of the Nativity in Bethlehem, also kindled popular interest in them. The first object of exploration naturally was Jerusalem itself. And the first explorers were officers of the Royal Engineers of the British Army: Sir Charles Wilson and Sir Charles Warren. Later Colonel Conder and Lieutenant Herbert Kitchener, the future Field Marshal, combining military interests with antiquarian, carried out a survey of the country west of the Jordan, and produced accurate maps of it. They marked the names of the villages, the streams, the mountains and the sites of ruins. Sir Charles Warren began the excavation of the ancient walls of the City of Jerusalem. He dug an exploratory tunnel and shaft outside the wall of the Moslem sacred enclosure, the Haram, which occupied the site of Solomon's and of Herod's Temple. It is striking that eighty years later—in 1954—a large stretch of that wall was uncovered when Arabs were building a road outside the walled city. By that time the lines of the three hills of the Holy City, Mount Moriah, Mount Zion and Mount Ophel, and the lines of the walls of King David and the Kings of Judah, of Herod, the Roman, and the Byzantine emperors, of the Arabs, the Crusaders and the Turks, had been delimited.

One of the decisive moments in the widening of knowledge was the discovery that the mounds (Tels) which were dotted over the plains and hills of Palestine, and were covered by fragments of pottery, marked buried cities or villages of antiquity. When explored, they would reveal to the excavator layer after layer of history and civilization. For in the little country it has been the practice of the conquerors to destroy the walls, temples and principal buildings of the captured town or fortress, and then on the rubble to build another town and a new wall, but leaving the foundations, and often much more, buried beneath the destruction. A further basis of accurate knowledge was laid when the most famous of the English archaeologists

The New Old Land of Israel

who worked in Palestine and Egypt from the end of the 19th century, the late Sir Flinders Petrie, proved that the pottery vessels, jars, jugs, vases, etc. and the pottery fragments, which were strewn on and under every Tel, could by their decoration, shape, and ornament be a sure guide not only to the historical events but to the movements of peoples and conquerors through the land. The least valuable objects yielded the most knowledge. Baked clay is the most abundant and the most imperishable of all the products of human art and craft. It is also the most easily transported. So the domestic vessels and lamps of one country are brought to another, and left behind, and can be distinguished from the native ware by their colour, marking, or ornament. Comparison of the pottery found in ancient sites in Palestine, Greece, and the Mediterranean islands, in Iraq, Asia Minor (Anatolia), and Egypt, could then reveal the intercourse between the peoples of those countries. And it was proved that the world of Antiquity in the Eastern Mediterranean and the Middle East was, like the modern world, international. Movement and communication of peoples in the 18th or 14th centuries B.C. was not much less than in the 14th or 18th centuries A.D. And so far as we know there were no passports or visas.

Pottery reflected the changes of political events and artistic trends. Moreover, by careful examination of the pieces, the layers of the mound in which the sherds (fragments of pottery) and the clay vessels were lying could be dated with almost scientific precision. In that way a chronology of the Near and Middle East could be built up. Pottery could make another valuable contribution to the knowledge of antiquity. Examination of every piece, perfect and imperfect, often revealed written signs, letters and words, sometimes inscribed, sometimes written in two or more languages. Some of them were in Hebrew, and often in an early script like the Phoenician. Each level of the mound was like the shelf of a bookcase: the top shelf being the record of the last inhabitants.

The history of antiquity is thus built up from a mass of little

The Archaeology of the Land of Israel

objects left in destroyed towns by the conquerors. The main periods of civilization in the Bible lands are distinguished not only by the different types of pottery, but by the use of metals. Stone was the material of the first instruments and weapons. The invention of the potter's wheel and the making of jars and pots goes back to near 5000 B.C. The Calcholithic (copper-stone) age, 4500—3200, marks the transition from stone to metal. The Early Bronze age, when copper began to be worked on a large scale, runs from 3200—2000; the Middle Bronze age from 2000—1500; the Late Bronze from 1500—1200; and the iron age from 1200.

The fuller knowledge of the land and the times of the Bible was interpreted in the latter part of the 19th century by a brilliant Scottish divine and professor of Theology, Sir George Adam Smith, Principal of Aberdeen University. A comparison of his book, the Historical Geography of the Holy Land, with Robinson's Geography of Palestine, mentioned above, shows the larger understanding which a generation of scholars and explorers had created. After more than 50 years that book remains a classic guide to the Bible story, even though countless additions have been made in the meantime to the archaeology of the region.

During this century archaeology has become more and more scientific. It is no longer enough to sink a shaft or dig a trench in an ancient site. The whole mound, or at least a large section of it is uncovered, layer by layer, till the expedition reaches rock bottom. Every wall and chamber, floor and hole, and every object found in the layer is carefully examined, described, and compared with the record of other sites in the Middle East. Only after the upper layers, which are the later in time, have been searched, measured and plotted, does the expedition proceed to dig the more ancient courses.

The first complete excavation of a Palestinian Tel was made in the first years of the century (1902-9), in a mound situated in the Judean hills, which had been identified with Gezer. That

The New Old Land of Israel

fortress town is frequently mentioned in the Bible, in the book of Joshua and Judges, and in the story of Solomon; and it was part of the dowry given by the Pharaoh to Solomon's Egyptian wife. It was mentioned also in the inscribed story and richly sculpted monuments of the Assyrian Sennacherib's and the Babylonian Nebuchadnezzar's, invasions of Canaan, and in the written record of the Maccabean wars (160—130 B.C.). It was a very ancient site inhabited by prehistoric men. Professor Macalister, who carried out the work for the Palestine Exploration Fund, uncovered not only temples of the Canaanites and Egyptians, and records in cuneiform, and one of the earliest Hebrew inscriptions, but also remains of a remoter past of cave-dwellers who had constructed a subterranean water tunnel.

Another Bible site which was thoroughly explored, as it was thought, in the early years of this century, was Jericho, in the lower part of the Jordan valley. German scholars dug deep into the mound, which lay outside the modern village, by a copious spring; and believed that they had revealed all its secrets and confirmed the Bible story. The more thorough knowledge and better methods of our own day have proved that the most sensational relics of an age much older than that of the Exodus of Israel from Egypt and of Joshua's invasion of Canaan had escaped their notice.

A third scientific expedition was conducted by Americans in the hill country during the Ottoman regime before the First World War. It worked on the ruins of the biblical Samaria, which was the capital city of the Kingdom of Israel, and is now in the Kingdom of Jordan. That digging, too, brought great addition to knowledge of the Bible; for, besides the walls and relics of temples and royal palaces, they found pottery sherds stamped with Hebrew names, and pieces of ivory, inlaid, painted and sculpted, which were identified with the ivory couches of King Ahab and his Phoenician Queen Jezebel that the Prophet Amos denounced. The deliverance of Palestine from the Turks and the conferment of a British Mandate over the country opened an era of intense exploration. Not only

The Archaeology of the Land of Israel

British societies but those of Europe and America were encouraged to send expeditions. And by the munificence of the American John Rockefeller junior, a museum worthy of the country and of the new discoveries was built in Jerusalem to preserve and display the treasures. Everything of primary importance for the knowledge of antiquity that was dug up was housed in it. The expeditions were no longer permitted to take away the spoil. The British mandatory government, however, unlike its Ottoman predecessor, gave every encouragement and help to the scientific expeditions. It was no longer necessary to dig a deep trench, explore it as rapidly as possible, and then cover up the site. A large area or a complete Tel could be systematically dug and examined yard by yard, without haste, over a period of years.

In the twenty-eight years of the British Mandate, despite many setbacks through local troubles and the Arab revolt 1936-9, and the interruption of the Second World War, unparalleled strides were made in the march of discovery of civilization from the dawn of mankind to our own age. The most historical of lands became an open-air museum. First, a big new chapter, the Annals of Prehistoric Man, was written from the exploration of the caves in the coastal plain of Palestine and in the valley of Jordan, which were among the earliest dwellings of the human race. The hills were riddled with natural caves, and ample supplies of flint were available for the making of tools and weapons. Mr Turville-Petre picked up in 1925, in a cave near the Sea of Galilee, a skull of a primitive man not less than 30,000 years old. The caves of Mount Carmel provided abundant material from which to identify the stage at which food-gathering man began systematically to cultivate the soil and establish villages, about 8,000 B.C. During the Neolithic (that is, New Stone) Age, which followed, till 4,500 B.C. man learned in increasing numbers to cultivate cereals and to prepare grain. The arts of animal husbandry, of the potter's wheel, and of the building of stone or mud-huts were practised. The beginning of the use of metal followed in the Calcholithic

The New Old Land of Israel

Age. Man learnt to smelt copper for use in tools, weapons and ornaments; and gradually metal superseded stone. The plough was invented. Houses of brick replaced mud-walled huts. And their plastered walls were decorated, sometimes with geometric patterns, sometimes with pictures of animals and human beings.

A remarkable group of English women scholars, led by Professor Dorothy Garrod of Cambridge, and including Miss Jacquetta Hopkins (Hawkes), who later won fame by her books on the geology and archaeology of Britain, were pioneers in this archaeology of prehistoric man. The British Administration in the twenties proposed to quarry stone for the building of the Haifa harbour from caves on the West side of Mount Carmel. The Department of Antiquities of the Palestine Government, concerned lest precious records of history should be irretrievably ruined for the sake of cheap stone, then carried out a survey of the caves. They lighted on a mass of flint instruments, stone mortars and pestles; and amongst them the remarkable carving of a bull's head in stone; and that induced the thorough search conducted by modern woman seeking primitive man. The caves yielded not only a series of human burials and skeletons from a necropolis at least twenty thousand years old, but also a number of works of art and craft; the carving of a young deer, a man's head, and a store of agricultural and fishing instruments. Many skeletons were decorated with necklace and headdress of shells. The layers of the caves were like the layers of the Tels, representing different periods of pre-history. In these Athlit caves the top levels were occupied 20,000 B.C., but the bottom layers went back perhaps to 100,000. The caves compared with those that have been revealed in France of the Magdalenian Age.

About the same time as the English-women were exploring the caves of the Carmel, a French archaeologist-Consul, M. Neuville, was exploring caves near Bethlehem. He found carvings and drawings of wild animals, elephant, hippopotamus, rhinoceros, which formed a frieze on the walls. The rude draw-

The Archaeology of the Land of Israel

ings, tricked out by black paint, depicted the life of an age when the culture and the climate of Palestine were very different from to-day. Later he dug mounds on the East side of Jordan beyond Jericho, and uncovered the ruins of human habitations which marked the progress from cave-dwelling to town-dwelling. The digging indicated that, between 7,000 and 4,000 years before the common era, the lower Jordan valley was an alluvial plain dotted with small towns. Men lived in rectangular houses built on stone foundations, the walls made of reeds smeared with mud. The absence of a more advanced culture on the site seemed to confirm the Bible story of a destruction of 'the Cities of the Plain' in the time of the Patriarch Abraham.

Another major discovery in the Bible lands during this period was the written record of half a dozen languages which had been hidden mysteries for centuries. Whole libraries were uncovered in excavations by French scholars in Northern Syria, then under French Mandate. The area was near the port of Latakia, which was a famous harbour both in Antiquity and in the Middle Ages. The most sensational discoveries were made in mounds by the shore which were identified with the site of the ancient Phoenician city of Ugarit. The languages included Sumerian and Accadian, which were the oldest written tongues of Chaldea (Mesopotamia); Hittite, belonging to a people of Central Asia which migrated and conquered a great part of the Middle East between 1,600 and 1,200 B.C.; Phoenician, of the sea-going people who occupied the Syrian coast; and the most ancient Hebrew. They were all written in a cuneiform script and largely on clay tablets. To understand the importance of the discoveries we must interpose a short account of the development of Semitic writing.

The earliest script which has been deciphered is that of the clay tablets of Mesopotamia, going back perhaps to 4,000 B.C. They are partly in pictographic signs, which were written with a stylus on the soft material. Coherent clay suitable for the purpose was abundant in the alluvial soil, and after the inscription was made it could be dried in the sun. Later it was baked

The New Old Land of Israel

in an oven, to eliminate the possibility of change or falsification. That form of writing is known as cuneiform, meaning wedgelike, because it was executed with a kind of wedge action in the clay. It was adapted by the scribes to the syllabic writing of the Accadian language, and gradually the signs lost the resemblance to the objects which they originally depicted. While clay tablets were the commonest material, hard stone, which had to be chiselled, and metals which had to be cut, were used for the most solemn records. So the famous code of law of the Babylonian king Hammurabi (about 2,000 B.C.) in four thousand lines was inscribed on a solid block of Diorite.

In Egypt a thousand years later the priests of the temples developed another form of pictorial writing, which we know as hieroglyphs. Each of the characters represented an object, a bird, a house, etc. While the commonest writing material there was the fibre of the papyrus plant, which grew plentifully in the Nile valley, clay tablets were also freely employed for official documents, and the most solemn records of all, telling of the achievements of the Pharaohs, were sculpted on huge stone obelisks and on magnificent pylons and the walls of the temples.

At Ugarit the archives of the library, though in half a dozen languages, were all in various cuneiforms. But the Phoenician and the most ancient Hebrew scripts already had alphabetic signs. The invention of an alphabet, in which each sign represents a sound and not an object, is one of the most precious contributions of the Semitic peoples to humanity. In place of the cumbrous machinery of ideograms and syllabic script, with over 600 characters, the Semites conceived the epochmaking invention that each sound should be expressed by one sign. The library of Ugarit, which can be dated from the middle of the second millennium B.C., illustrates the experimental transition from picture language to alphabet. Whether it was the Phoenician or other Semitic tribes—some suggest the Habiri, ancestors of the Hebrews—who devised the first alphabet—cannot be said. It does seem certain, however, that the Phoenician

The Archaeology of the Land of Israel

traders developed this ready method of recording their accounts and mercantile transactions; and that they carried the alphabet to the West through their contacts with the Greek peoples. And so they played a constructive part in Western civilization. Copies of the Ugarit alphabet of thirty letters—all consonants —found on the site have much the same order as the later Hebrew alphabet. One copy was made by an apprentice scribe who wrote each letter seven times for practice. Another tablet includes, by the side of each alphabetic letter, a syllabic character of the Mesopotamian language. Scholars have conjectured that the Nomad Hebrews brought the Sumerian language to Canaan, mixed it there with the Canaanite tongue, and adopted the Phœnician alphabetic script.

Before the uncovering of the cuneiform libraries of Ugarit, archaeologists in the early years of this century found in the Sinai peninsula many rough inscriptions on stone. They have not yet been read with certainty, but the form of the signs seems to mark a stage between the Egyptian hieroglyphs and the Semitic alphabet. The finds in this region of archaic writing that goes back at least to the middle of the second millennium B.C. have confounded the Bible higher critics of a previous generation, who were sceptical about Moses and the earlier Prophets having written the Mosaic Law and their messages. We now know for certain that, well before the date of the Exodus of Israel from Egypt, men wrote readily, and some of their earliest writing is found in the wilderness of Sinai where the Children of Israel wandered.

The early Semitic script of the tablets of Ugarit is found also, as we shall see, in inscribed records on pottery and on metal weapons of Gezer, Lachish and Megiddo. It was the regular Hebrew script till the time of the Babylonian captivity; and by a deliberate archaism was used for the Jewish coins of the second kingdom and the Maccabees. In our own day it has been the model for the wording of the postage stamps of the State of Israel. The later Hebrew alphabet, which has been used as the holy script since the Babylonian captivity, is the Aramaic,

The New Old Land of Israel

(i.e. Syrian: Aram being the Hebrew name of that country) which is also the parent of Arabic and Syriac writing. The square 'Assyrian' Hebrew letters, to-day used exclusively for the writing of the scrolls of the Law for the synagogue, came from that family.

Ugarit was one of the chief harbours of Northern Phoenicia, and one of the earliest meeting places of civilization. It was a terminus of caravan routes from Asia Minor, Syria and Mesopotamia. Visible from Cyprus, it was, too, a market where the merchants of the Aegean came to meet the merchants of Asia. The copper of that island was a great article of trade. The local civilization was Canaanite, and the tablets found in the temples give us a written record of their religion in epic poems by Oriental Homers. The Canaanite Baal is the principal figure; but there are other gods and goddesses, among them Elohim, who in the Hebrew Bible is a synonym of Jehovah, Dagon and Reshef, who also are mentioned in the Bible among the Philistine pagan worships. Daniel appears as a god of wisdom and justice, who judges the cases of the widow and the orphan. A religious epic in six hundred lines tells of a struggle between Baal and Moth. The documents make mention also of the people, Habiri, who are found in Egyptian documents of the fifteenth century. Some scholars identify them with the Hebrews; the most accepted theory today is that the name means nomads, and was generic. The Hebrews of the Exodus of the Bible, led by Moses and Joshua, were a part of the Nomad race. The most recent diggings at Ugarit uncovered, next to the royal palace, houses of the 14th and 13th centuries B.C., which are equipped with bath-rooms and drainage, indicating an advanced civilization. The houses would seem to have been occupied by the scribes and clerks of the court, because many word-lists were found in them. Beneath the houses were burial vaults sealed with molten lead poured into the crevices of the stone. They had been pillaged by tomb-robbers, but not thoroughly. Many golden ornaments, alabaster vases, bronze arms, and painted terracotta vases were found in them. In the houses

The Archaeology of the Land of Israel

were a hundred or more clay tablets, or fragments of tablets, which were part of dictionaries; and also letters addressed to the kings of Ugarit from the rulers of other countries. Some of these latest dictionary tablets contained four columns of words, in the Sumerian and Accadian, and also in the Ugaritic, and what is called Hurrite language spoken in North Syria. The Hurrite script is the Accadian syllabary, while the Ugaritic is alphabetical, and close to Hebrew. Like Hebrew and all other Semitic alphabets the letters represent only consonants. The vowels must be supplied by the reader.

Another civilization of a biblical people, the Hittites, has been revealed in Syria and Palestine by the archaeologists. They came from Central Asia to Northern Syria, and made their way to the hilly country of Canaan in the century before the Children of Israel entered the Holy Land. Their mingling with the Canaanites and the Hebrews is symbolized in the verse of the Prophet Ezekiel about Jerusalem:—'Thy father was an Amorite, and thy mother was a Hittite' (Ez.16.3.). The name of the governor of Jerusalem Abd-Khiba, of the fourteenth century, who appears in the Egyptian documents of Amarna (see page 33), is part Hittite, Khiba being a Hittite goddess.

In the period of the British Mandate for Palestine, some of the Tels which were famous Bible sites, and had already been surveyed or superficially excavated, e.g. Megiddo and Baisan (Beth Shaan), were thoroughly explored. The explorations threw a flood of light on the passage of the conquerors along the military highway between Africa and Asia, between Egypt and Syria. Using modern methods, removing the layers of ruin systematically, and examining every object which came to hand, the explorers were able to rewrite the history of the Land of the Bible and the people of the Bible with a fuller knowledge and a clearer insight than was vouchsafed in any previous age.

The most spectacular find, indeed, was due not to the digging of the scientific expeditions but to the chance roamings of Bedu-Arab shepherds. In 1947, when Palestine was in turmoil

The New Old Land of Israel

and the British Mandate was approaching its end, two of the illiterate children of the desert, chasing their goats, broke into a cave near the Dead Sea, in a region which seemed utterly remote from civilization. In those caves they found deposited in jars leather scrolls which, when read by the scholars, proved to be books of the Hebrew Bible and of apocryphal and apocalyptic literature that were written before the Christian era. The hunt, which was then started by Beduin as well as by scholars, for records of the past in the desert region has not yet ended. It has already given us undreamt of documents that, by their age and their contents, profoundly affect the previous conceptions of Jewish and early Christian life and letters. The documents were written in the troubled era when the Jews were fighting a life and death struggle with the Romans, and Judaism was in constant and irreconcilable conflict with the Hellenistic-Roman culture. The discoveries have brought home to the common man the new knowledge, which has been so skilfully gathered, of the continuity of civilization in the Bible lands.

Since the scrolls were found, little Palestine has been divided into two separate and—hitherto—hostile states; and the communication between scholars living on the two sides of the frontiers has been interrupted. That perverse situation has at least provoked a healthy emulation between the scholars. Jewish archaeologists have pursued their searches in the territory of Israel, and have carried out a number of enterprises simultaneously, in Jerusalem itself and in the seabord by Tel-Aviv and Acre, in the hills of Galilee and in Caesarea, in the desert spaces of the Negev, and by the shores of the Dead Sea. English, European and American expeditions have at the same time pursued their searches in the wilderness of Judaea—which is within the Arab territory of Jordan—for more records that may be incredibly preserved. They have made, too, fresh discoveries in the mounds of Jericho that carry back the proof of civilization and of man's earliest art and artifice to 8,000 years before the Christian era. The last years since the establishment

The Archaeology of the Land of Israel

of the State of Israel have, against all expectation, been the most productive of knowledge of the past of the Children of Israel and the Jewish people.

The written record of Antiquity in Israel, apart from the books of the Bible, was slender in quantity till the extraordinary finds of the latest years. Papyrus, which is almost imperishable in rainless Egypt, quickly perished in the climate of Palestine. And very few papyrus records have been found in the Land of Israel. Long inscriptions on stone, too, which are common in the imperial countries, Egypt, Assyria and Babylon, recording the great deeds of the conquerors, are almost unknown. Canaan was materially a poor country compared with the lands of the great rivers, the Nile, the Euphrates and the Orontes; and the objects discovered have been for the most part of small intrinsic and artistic value. Nothing splendid like the tombs of the Kings of Egypt at Thebes, or of the Kings of Chaldaean Ur, or of Mycenaean Argos. have come from Jerusalem, Jericho or Samaria. What, however, is distinctive of Israel archaeology is the continuous picture of human endeavour from the dawn of civilization through the ages.

Israel are to-day a people of the spade as well as a people of the Book. Pages of the Bible spring to life as the archaeologists supply fresh knowledge and fresh interpretations, and the struggles of the Hebrews against the empires of Antiquity are reflected in the struggle of Israel to-day with the neighbouring Arab States, and often on the very same scene. The mass interest of the Israelis, whatever their country of origin, in the widespread archaeological activity is stimulated by patriotic feeling. They sense a mystic connection with the past of the Children of Israel and with the visible evidence of ancient Hebrew civilization in the land. The army of Israel has archaeology instructors, and archaeology is a compulsory subject for officers. The first task of a new settlement is to start digging up the past at the same time as they dig for the future. And the excavations of the past are laid out as lovingly as the new cultivated fields.

The New Old Land of Israel

I may give one example out of many from personal experience. On the frontier of Jordan in the Samarian foothills, the Israel Army planted a few years ago a 'colony', in the old Roman sense. That is a group of young soldiers, male and female, who establish a new agricultural village, and at the same time keep watch and ward. When we visited it, the post had no name, just a number; but the continuity of civilization in every corner of the land was brought home at once. We were told that in the past week a group who were digging an irrigation ditch came across signs of an ancient building. They had exposed a corner of a mosaic floor, and an archaeologist of the Government department was at once called in. He uncovered an impressive piece of Byzantine craftsmanship. Here was the site of a Christian monastery of the early centuries; and he identified it with a village a thousand years older, which is mentioned in the Bible, and was recorded on a potsherd found in Samaria by other archaeologists twenty years earlier. A ruined Arab hamlet on the other side of the frontier line still bears the name corresponding with the Hebrew name on the potsherd. So the military post of present Israel was put on the site of a town of the Kingdom of Ahab and of the Byzantine Empire.

The Israelis to-day are everywhere eager to preserve the visible remains of their forbears as a local monument. Besides the local societies, a fellowship of amateur antiquarians has sprung up; and it is a coveted office to be the honorary warden of an ancient site. The Ministry of Education and Culture includes a Department of Antiquities, and has taken the responsibility for the conservation of ancient ruins. It has established in Jewish Jerusalem a temporary museum, supplementing the Rockefeller Museum of Arab Jerusalem, which for the time is inaccessible to Jews. In a few years it has collected a remarkable treasure from the two hundred and fifty excavations of ancient sites which have been made in all parts of Israel since 1948.

Goethe wrote that a man who cannot give an account

The Archaeology of the Land of Israel

of 3,000 years dwells in darkness. The Israelis, returning after nearly 2,000 years to their old home, are conscious of 4,000 years of history behind them. The discovery of Antiquity has a religious appeal to many who have given up the traditional observances of Judaism. It gives them a root in the past of their people and a link of continuity.

II

Jerusalem

JERUSALEM, so Disraeli said, is a city where heaven and earth meet. Poets have written more about it, and painters have depicted it more, than any other place in the world. What gives the city the unique character? First, there is the physical setting. It is built on a high part of a limestone plateau, nearly three thousand feet above the Mediterranean Sea on the West, and over four thousand feet above the Dead Sea on the East. Between the city and the coastal plain of Palestine there stretch the austere rocky mountains of Judea. Between the city and the deep valley and abyss of the Jordan are the arid tortured folds of the wilderness of Judea; and beyond the valley and the Dead Sea, the mountain wall of Gilead and Moab rises higher than the mountains of Judea. Wrapped by day in a mystic blue haze, at dawn and dusk the mountain wall is lit with all the colours of nature.

The city of Jerusalem has been isolated from the highways throughout its 4,000 years of history. It is built on a remote plateau of the Judean hills, on the three peaks of Moriah, Zion and Ophel. The original town rose on the last and least celebrated of the three, Ophel, which means 'the hump'. Moriah means 'the vision of God': and Zion means 'the strong place'. Moriah was the site of the Temple of Solomon, of the second Temple, of Zerubbabel, built after the return from the captivity of Babylon, and of the third Temple, of Herod, which was rebuilt when the Jewish nation was already struggling for independence against the giant pagan power of Rome. That

2. New buildings of the Hebrew University

Mount Zion, overlooking the Old City. The domes to the right are on the site of Solomon's Temple

3. *Above*
Ossuary of the second temple period found in Jerusalem

Right: Third wall of Jerusalem built in the first century and a suburb of the twentieth

Jerusalem

Temple and the city of Jerusalem were destroyed by the legions of Rome in the first century of the Christian era. Zion was the site of the palaces of the Kings from David to Herod.

Jerusalem, on the three hills, was separated from the surrounding plateau by sheer deep ravines, the Kidron valley and the vale of Jehosaphat in the East and the South: Hinnom (Gehenna) on the West. Only on the north side was it linked with the tableland of the central range of Palestine. The invader regularly approached on that side. When Jerusalem enters the Bible story, in the books of Joshua and Judges, it was a fortress of a Canaanite people, the Jebusites, and had also the name of Jebus. In the Book of Judges it is said: 'The Children of Israel did not drive out the inhabitants of Jerusalem', implying that there was at first no complete conquest. The Hebrew name, Yerushalaim, is grammatically a dual form; and probably there were two cities then as now. In the period before David's conquest one was occupied by the tribe of Judah, the other by the Jebusites. To-day similarly one part is occupied by the Jews, who from all parts of the world have immigrated, mostly during the last half-century: the other by the Arabs, who were the majority of the inhabitants of the country before the creation of the State of Israel.

Jerusalem, indeed, like other cities of ancient Israel, appears in recorded history in Egyptian diplomatic documents of the 14th century B.C. These documents are clay tablets with cuneiform writing of the Accadian language, which was the diplomatic lingua franca. They were found in the latter part of the 19th century beneath a mound in the Egyptian Delta, Tel El Amarna. The mound covered the city and palace of the reforming Pharaoh, Akhenaton (c. 1380), who reigned just after the period of the Exodus of Israel—if the general opinion of the scholars is correct. The Egyptian dominion over Mesopotamia, Syria and Palestine, established by the conquering Pharaohs of the previous century, was breaking up; and the vassals of Egypt in the strong places of the conquered lands addressed their requests for help to their suzerain lord in his capital. Abdkhiba was the ruler of Jerusalem, which appears as the capital city of Southern Palestine (Canaan). He writes that he is slandered, because he reproached the King's officer with favouring the Habiri—invaders, who may be the Hebrews, 'Let troops be sent; for the King has no longer any territory. The Habiri have wasted all'. And he adds an earnest appeal to the scribe of the King: 'Bring aloud before my Lord the words:— The whole territory of the King is going to ruin'.

Water is the prime need for settled habitation in the Orient, and Jerusalem has its perennial spring. The city of the Jebusites and of David grew around two springs in the valley. One was Gihon, mentioned in the Hebrew Bible, which burst out under the rock at the bottom of Ophel, and was later called the Virgin's Pool. The other was the pool of Siloam, which lies to the south-east, down the Vale of the Kidron, and is described by the English poet Milton as 'Siloah's Brook, which flows past the oracles of God'. The springs gave, and still give, water for the inhabitants of the city and for the cultivation of the limestone slopes. The cities of antiquity were fantastically small on our modern scale; they were designed primarily for defence, and comprised a few acres enclosed with a strong wall. Ophel, the city captured by David, was 400 yards long and 300 yards broad. His general, Joab, scaled an underground water-course and took the Jebusite garrison by surprise, and later David built a bastion to the wall to make it stronger. The bastion was unearthed thirty years ago by British archaeologists working in an area which lies outside the present walls of Jerusalem, and was then covered by market gardens. In 1954 other archaeologists, digging in the Kidron valley between David's bastion and the Mount of the Temple, which is enclosed by the medieval wall, uncovered the foundations of a much older wall and of a gate which must have belonged to the city of David.

David, the warrior king, marked Mount Moriah for the sanctuary of the Children of Israel, the place where the Ark of the Covenant should have its permanent abode. There the one universal God should be worshipped without any graven

Jerusalem

image. He purchased the threshing-floor on the hill for the site of the Temple, but his hands were stained with blood, and he left it to his son, Solomon, the Wise King, to build the shrine. Himself he placed his palace and fortress on the third hill, Zion, which dominated the others. The Citadel of David is still the name of a strong place on Zion, which was the Turkish military headquarters within the walled city, in the years of the British Mandate the principal police post, and more recently a post of the Jordan Army.

Archaeologists have proved that the foundations of the tower are part of the castle Phasael built by King Herod, and the lower courses of the building go back to the time of the Maccabees. To-day the Citadel is a barrack in the Arab city, by the main gate in the walls which the Jews call the Jaffa Gate. The Arabs know it as the Gate of the Friend, because the road leads from it to Hebron, which is the city of the 'Friend of God', the Patriarch Abraham.

David chose Jerusalem for the capital of his kingdom because of its central strategic position. Hebron, which was then a bigger city and also a holy place, was too far to the South. He chose it after his victory over the Philistines in the Vale of Rephaim which lies below Mount Zion. We associate the Philistines with the coastal plain. But stones inscribed with the signet of Philistine officers were found in recent years on the outskirts of the city of Jerusalem in the vale, and a scarab of Ramases III, who in the 12th century defeated the people of the Sea, i.e. the Philistines. The imperial Pharaoh settled them, it seems, in the hill-country as a frontier defence force. And when the power of Egypt declined in the days of the Judges of Israel, the Philistines contended with the Hebrew tribes for mastery in the hills as well as in the plains. In the same Vale of Rephaim the first Jewish suburb outside the walls was built one hundred years ago through the benevolence of Sir Moses Montefiore, the great-hearted Anglo-Jewish philanthropist and precursor of Zionism, who dedicated his efforts to settlement of Jews from the Holy towns on the soil.

The New Old Land of Israel

David's and Solomon's tombs are traditionally a holy place, close to the Citadel, and on the pinnacle of Mount Zion, but just outside the Turkish Walls. Nebi Daoud, (i.e. Tomb of David), as the Arabs called it, was a Moslem Shrine; and an upper chamber, the reputed scene of the Last Supper of Jesus, was a Christian shrine. The Holy Place was barred to the Jews till the War of Independence 1948. Then the Israel Army captured this strong-point, and drove out the Arab forces. The Tomb of David, in the lower chamber of the Mosque, was turned from a Moslem to a Jewish holy place. It has become during the last years a principal place of prayer and worship for inhabitants and Jewish visitors, who cannot for the time being visit the holiest of all the sites for Jews in Jerusalem. That is the Western Wall of the Temple, the Kotel Maaravi, vulgarly called the Jews' Wailing Wall, which is in the heart of the Old City, and being in the Arab area, inaccessible since 1948 to Jews.

The Temple of Solomon, of which this was the outer wall, was the glory of the nation. The peak of Mount Moriah was levelled to make a broad platform; the cedars of the structure—for the building was of wood—were brought from the mountains of Lebanon; the craftsmen for decorating the sanctuary were brought from Phoenician Tyre, the gold for the holy vessels from Ophir, the copper from the mines in the Negev. Of the First Temple two relics remain in Jerusalem of to-day; the section of the Western Wall, built of square blocks of stone, and the slab of rock which was the altar for the sacrifices, and traditionally also the place where the patriarch Abraham offered up his son Isaac. The place of the Temple is sacred to Moslem Arabs, who claim to be the sons of Ishmael, and thus descended from Abraham. Over the rock one of the most lovely shrines of the world was built by the Caliph Abdul Malik in the eighth century.* The vast sub-structures under the platform,

---

* Its Arabic name means 'Dome of the Rock'; but it is commonly, though wrongly, called The Mosque of Omar, the Moslem-Arab conqueror of Jerusalem.

Jerusalem

known as the Stables of Solomon, are probably of the age of Herod. The Stables of Solomon may have been used for the horses and chariots of that King; but more certainly were used by the Crusader Knights during the period of the Latin Kingdom.

In another part of Jerusalem vast underground galleries are known as the Quarries of King Solomon. Tradition has it that the stone for the outer Walls of the Temple was hewn from this part of the lime-stone hills. And the Freemasons of all countries hold the place in high regard.

In the archaeological annals of Jerusalem the next milestone, so to say, after the Temple is an inscription recording the making by King Hezekiah of the water-tunnel under Mount Moriah at the time of the Assyrian invasion by Sennacherib. In the Book of Isaiah we read how the King of Judah, fearing that the supply of water from the spring Gihon would be cut off by the invaders in the siege of the capital, ordered the excavation of a tunnel which would lead the water of the two springs, Gihon and Siloam, under the fortress, whence it could be drawn through a shaft for the inhabitants of the city. Sennacherib boasted in an inscription at his palace at Nineveh, which has survived, that he locked up the king of Judah 'like a bird in a cage'. But he had to raise the siege, and the tunnel has remained intact through the ages. About seventy years ago the French Consul in Jerusalem, M. Clermont Ganneau, who was also an enthusiastic archaeologist, heard that an Arab boy, wading through the tunnel, had come across an inscribed tablet in the roof of the passage and had removed it. He was able to get possession of it and to read the writing, which was an ancient Hebrew script. The legend recorded the meeting of the two parties of workers who were excavating the rock to build the tunnel. They heard the sound of pick on pick, and they marked the length and the depth of the passage. The tablet, thus amazingly preserved, is almost the earliest continuous writing in Hebrew which has survived. It is now in the Museum of Constantinople, and the Museum of Jerusalem has to be content

The New Old Land of Israel

with a squeeze facsimile. The Pool of Hezekiah, to which the king conducted the water for the inhabitants of the city, remains in the heart of old Jerusalem, between the Tower of David and the Church of the Sepulchre.

About a hundred years after the death of Hezekiah, Jerusalem was again besieged, by Nebuchadnezzar of Babylon. This time the city and the kingdom fell. The Prophet Jeremiah, who lived in a village of Anatoth, a few miles East of Jerusalem on the borders of the wilderness of Judaea—the village is today inhabited by Arabs—prophesied that the King would bring destruction on his people if he persisted in his alliance with Egypt against the new power from the East. He was thrown into prison for spreading alarm and despondency, and tradition has marked the place of his dungeon. It is a cave in a grotto outside the wall on the North side. His warning was justified by the event. Solomon's Temple was destroyed, the King and leaders of the people were killed or taken into captivity, and the city was left desolate. One of the royal family, however, Gedalia, was appointed by the conqueror to be governor of the remnant who remained. Of him we have recently recovered historic trace. A signet ring bearing his name was found in the excavation of Lachish, which was the outer fortress for the defence of Judaea.

Another surprising discovery from the days of Isaiah is a tomb in the Kidron Valley of which the inscription was only deciphered in recent years. It is the Tomb of Shebna, who was the steward of the royal household. (Isaiah 22.15).

The Babylon Empire lasted only half a century, and then the new Power of the Medes and the Persians arose in the Middle East, and founded an empire which lasted two centuries. Fifty years after the fall of Jerusalem the Persian King Cyrus proclaimed the invitation to the Jews of the captivity to return to the Land of Israel, and restore their national home and the Temple of the Universal God. Zerubbabel in 516 B.C., led a small host of fifty thousand who came from the rivers of Babylon 'as in a dream'. They rebuilt a shrine on the sacred Mount of

Jerusalem

Moriah, but it was a poor substitute for the glorious Temple of Solomon. Seventy years later, another Jewish leader, Nehemiah, who was high in favour of the Persian king, came to Jerusalem to direct the rebuilding of the walls of the city. The workers were molested by jealous bands of the Cutheans from Samaria —later known as the Samaritans—being remnants of the tribes of Israel mingled with the Assyrian people who were settled in the territory of Israel in the North. The Jews—as they were now called—worked with a trowel in one hand and a sword in the other. The line of Nehemiah's walls is minutely described in the Book of Ezra and Nehemiah, and many of the sites can be identified after 2,500 years.

Few monuments have been left in Jerusalem from the Persian period, those 200 years of peaceful history, because their building was overlaid in the more splendid Hellenistic-Roman era. But in the last years Jewish explorers, digging near the suburb of Ramat Rahel, the Southern outpost of the Jewish defence of Jerusalem in the War of Independence, 1948, uncovered a Tel which was hit in the shelling. Scholars identified it with the Biblical city of Netofa. That place is mentioned in the Book of Ezra and Nehemiah in connection with Bethlehem, and this site is close to the road from Jerusalem to Bethlehem. The diggers found jars marked with the Hebrew word Yahud, which was the Persian name for Judea, and with the Hebrew Yerushalaim.

An epoch-making turn in the history of Jerusalem was the conquest of the Persian Empire and all the Middle East by the King of Macedonia, Alexander the Great, in the latter part of the fourth century B.C. The contact of Greeks and Jews hitherto was that of traders on the coast, though a few intrepid travellers from Greece had made their way to Jerusalem and spread the tale of its imageless shrine to the Universal God. A Jewish legend recorded by Josephus, the historian of the first century A.D., tells how Alexander, who aspired to world empire, was so moved by the sublimity of the worship of the Universal God in Jerusalem that he refrained from entering the

The New Old Land of Israel

Holy of Holies. The High Priest of that time was Simon the Just, whose praises are sung in the Apocrypha book of Ecclesiasticus. His tomb under the Mount of Olives in Jerusalem was a place of annual pilgrimage for the Jews till 1948, but is now just outside the area of Israel, and inaccessible to them.

A large Hellenistic population finding Palestine—as they called it, from the Philistine coast which they first occupied—to be physically like their own country of Macedonia and Hellas, settled there and built cities. They gave Greek names to the cities and villages of Canaan; Acre became Ptolemais, Beth Shaan was Scythopolis, Amman across Jordan was Philadelphia. They built temples for their gods, colonnades for their schools, and gymnasia for their physical training and their games. They brought their Greek language and its noble literature. Two Greek dynasties, founded by Alexander's generals, long contended for Palestine after his death: the Ptolemies, whose capital was Alexandria in Egypt at the mouth of the Nile, and the Seleucids, whose capital was Antioch in the Syrian hills. The Ptolemies were tolerant; perhaps, they were admirers of Judaism. They encouraged the Jews to maintain their own way of life and to translate their holy writ into Greek tongue—the famous Septuagint version. The Seleucid emperors, who conquered the land at the beginning of the 2nd century B.C., were on the contrary, obsessed by the idea of religious homogeneity, and, stimulated by a section of the Jews who aped the culture of the ruling power and were ardent Hellenizers, sought to impose their pagan cults in the temple of Jerusalem, and built a gymnasium—the abomination of desolation—in the Holy City.

The religious tyranny provoked the heroic resistance of the Maccabees, the father and sons of a priestly family. The resistance, first organised in the village of Modin in the Judaean hills, grew to a revolt of the faithful among the people. In a few years Judaea was delivered by their prowess from the foreign yoke, and became an independent State, ruled by the Maccabean brothers in turn, and allied with the strong and growing power of Rome. The Temple was cleansed of the abominations,

Jerusalem

the city was fortified again with walls so that it could withstand attack; and the Maccabean princes by their prowess made themselves masters of a territory as great as that which had been ruled by David and Solomon. After a hundred years, however, of independence, the royal house was divided against itself; one of the contending princes called in the help of the Roman general Pompey, who was adding provinces in Asia to the Empire. Alliance was turned to dependence, and then to a yoke. For 200 years the Jewish people lived in conditions of constant revolt and perpetual mental strife, struggling against the hated suzerain power.

Yet Jerusalem, in the latter part of the 1st century B.C. was a town of great splendour. Herod the Great, King of Judea, of a family of Iduméa (Edom) which had been Judaised by the victorious Maccabean king, was a master-builder, and rivalled the Caesars themselves in the magnificence of his structures. In Jerusalem his supreme achievement was the rebuilding of the Temple, to make it one of the wonders of the world. Judaism was attracting converts by thousands in all parts of the Greek and Roman world; and thousands of the proselytes came to Jerusalem at the great festivals in pilgrimage. A few years ago, in the Mandate days, municipal workers, laying drains in the Old City of Jerusalem, lighted on a stone with inscriptions in Greek and Aramaic, warning the Gentiles not to pass beyond a point in the court of the Temple. The inner court was reserved for Jews. Besides the Temple, another and more popular place of worship and learning in this age was spread in Jerusalem and in all Jewish communities. That was the synagogue: a Greek word meaning place of assembly. Ruins of one dating from the first century B.C., were excavated in the oldest part of the city, on Ophel; and the inscription showed that, besides the synagogue, the donor had provided a hostel and bathrooms for pilgrims. The worship in the synagogue was without animal sacrifices: and a school—in Hebrew: 'house of study'—was regularly attached to it.

King Herod the Great built in the Greco-Roman style a massive sepulchre for his family on a hill opposite Mount Zion—the tomb-chambers, which are next to the King David Hotel, are still in good condition—; while for himself he built a tremendous burial-place in the bosom of a cone-shaped volcanic hill, East of Bethlehem, known today as the Frank Mountain, in the wilderness of Judea. Foreseeing the conflict with Rome, he built more forts to protect the city and to guard the Temple. Antonia, which covered the Temple, and three other towers were bastions in the circuit of the outer wall. The foundation of one of those towers is the base of the present citadel of David. Herod's grandson Agrippa continued that work, and shortly before the final struggle with Rome, built the 'Third Wall' of the city on the Northern side, where it was most exposed to attack. Large chunks of the wall have been uncovered in the northern and western suburbs. An exceptionally big stone-pillar, quarried for it, lies in the former Russian Pilgrim compound, outside the present walls, by the side of the building which since 1918 has accommodated, first Palestine's, and then Israel's Courts of Justice.

Of the same period are the ornate tombs in the valley of Jehosaphat or Kidron below the Mount of the Temple. They bear the name of Absalom, Zachariah, James, and are attributed to those Bible characters by popular legend. But they belong to the Herodian period. It was an age when magnificence was displayed in the monuments to the dead. From this last period of Jewish splendour, before the destruction of the state, we have in the Northern suburbs striking monuments known as the Tombs of the Kings. They have nothing to do with the Kings of Israel and Judah, but are the burial place dating from the 1st century of a Judaised princess from Mesopotamia and her family. Josephus tells of her love for Jerusalem and her direction that her and her sons' bodies should be laid to rest there. The tombs are ornate in the Hellenistic style, as are another group of Tombs of the Judges not far away. The judges, mostly unnamed, are the heads of the Sanhedrin in the last period of the Judaean State before the Jews were expelled

Jerusalem

from Jerusalem, and the tombs are in a quarter now named Sanhedria.

It was in this age that the story of the passion of Jesus was enacted in Jerusalem. Professor Sukenik, the archaeologist of the Hebrew University of Jerusalem discovered ossuaries in tomb-chambers on the road from Jerusalem to Bethlehem which were marked with the Christian cross. Among them was a casket of the Bar Saba Family which is mentioned in the Acts of the Apostles among the followers of Jesus. When Christianity became the religion of the Roman Empire in the 4th century, the city of Jerusalem excited such an outburst of religious devotion as no other place in the world has known. The traditional sites of the passion were marked with a church or basilica, or a monastery; and when in the Dark Ages the Church split into two rival communities, the western under the Pope of Rome and the eastern under the Byzantine Empire, each community set up its separate monument round its religious site. So we have at the foot of the Mount of Olives two Gardens of Gethsemane, each with its olive trees and each with its church. And within the Church of the Sepulchre there are many chapels of the different Christian churches. Greek Orthodox, Roman Catholic, Coptic, etc.

The siege of Jerusalem by the Roman Titus, and the destruction of the city and the Temple, changed the topography as well as the history of the city. A valley between Zion and Moriah was filled with the rubble of the ruins, so that it ceased to be a natural cleft. The hills to the West of the city were occupied by camps of the Roman legion. The village Colonia, a few miles on the road towards the sea, still keeps its Roman name; and recent excavations of a neighbouring hill for the building of a congress and convention hall exposed the lines and the signs of the Tenth Roman Legion. The record of the Roman triumph over the Jews was not erected in Jerusalem, but in Rome itself. The Arch of Titus there shows the Ark of the Covenant, the seven-branched candelabra and the shewbread carried by Jewish captives. The legend on the Arch

The New Old Land of Israel

runs:— 'He destroyed that Jerusalem which had been attacked in vain by warriors, by peoples and by kings, who could not approach her'. Nearly 1,900 years after it was built, Jewish soldiers, who were part of the Allied Forces then occupying Italy, celebrated in 1948, in the shadow of that arch, the restoration of the Jewish State.

After the crushing of the desperate revolt of Bar Cochba, sixty years later by the Emperor Hadrian, 135 A.D. (see Ch. 10.), the effort was made to blot out in Jerusalem the memory of the Jewish religion. On the site of the Temple Hadrian erected a shrine to Jupiter and a temple to Venus. The name of the pagan city was changed to the Latin, *Aelia Capitolina*. The Jews themselves were excluded from the place altogether, save on one day of the year, the 9th of Ab. On that anniversary of three destructions, they might come as a mark of their humiliation, and pour out their lamentation at the relic of the wall of the Temple.

Two hundred years later Jerusalem was rescued from its imposition of paganism, and became again venerated as the centre of a monotheist universal religion. Constantine, the emperor who routed the barbarians threatening the life of an empire which had been invincible for 400 years, and made a new capital at Byzantium on the borders of Europe and Asia, adopted for his state the religion which had stemmed from Judaism. Christianity henceforth was installed as an Imperial creed in the new capital, as well as in Rome and Jerusalem. Constantine's mother, Helena, a British princess and a devoted adherent of the Christian faith, made a pilgrimage to the Holy City. Having learned the tradition of the sites of the Crucifixion, the Burial and the Resurrection, she caused splendid churches and basilicas to be erected on them. A new Jerusalem was centred round the Church of the Sepulchre and the Via Dolorosa along the scenes of the Passion which led to it. Henceforth the cross and the steeple, the mosaics, the paintings and the sculptures of Jesus and the Apostles were multiplied in the city. For a brief period (361-3 A.D.) one of Constantine's suc-

Jerusalem

cessors, the Emperor Julian, having repudiated Christianity, invited the Jews to return to the city, rebuild their Temple, and clear out the Church which persecuted them. That was not to be: he was murdered, and all that recalls the episode is a road in the Jewish section of the city, known as Julian Way. We have a remarkable picture of Byzantine Jerusalem in a mosaic map—probably of the 6th century A.D.—which is preserved on the floor of a church in the village of Madeba across Jordan. Jerusalem is the centre of the map which depicted the whole of Palestine. The mosaic shows in detail the city walls, towers, churches and streets, and the Western Wall where the Jews prayed.

Jewish revolt against the Imperial and Church persecutors broke out time and again in the 4th and 5th centuries. The Persian King Chosroes, who captured Palestine and Jerusalem from the Romans in the 6th century, enrolled Jews in his forces. They were still a people of military prowess. But the struggle between Christian and Persian was quelled when the nomad Arabs, professing a new form of monotheism preached by Mohammed of Mecca, in an amazing half century overwhelmed both empires. They made Jerusalem a Moslem city, and the third holiest of a realm that stretched from the Atlantic to the Indian Ocean. The conquering Arabs of those ages were tolerant, and they allowed the peoples of the Book, the Jews and the Christians, to maintain their worship, their synagogues and their churches in the city. The Jews established their schools again, particularly on the Mount of Olives, from which they looked down on the place of the Temple now occupied by a Moslem shrine; and they buried their dead on the slopes of the mountain, which became a vast Jewish cemetery.

For their worship of Allah (the one universal God), the Moslems brought into the city a new form of prayer-place, the mosque, which had no altar, no choir, and no nave. They brought, too, a new form of calling the people to prayer in place of the Christian bells: the minaret, modelled on the lighthouse or watch-tower, from which the Crier (muezzin) proclaimed five times a day the greatness of God. The Arab Caliphs restored, too, the glory of the place of the Temple on Mount Moriah. We have remarked that the building, which is commonly known as the Mosque of Omar, was in fact built by the Caliph Abdul Malik in the 8th century. Noting the greatness of the Dome of the Church of the Sepulchre, and the magnificence of the Church, he resolved to erect a building which should rival the Christian. It was not a mosque, but a dome built over the rock of the sacrifice of Abraham and the altar of the Temple. Its octagonal structure became the model of many of the Christian churches in Europe. The Knights of the Temple, the Templars, in the times of the Crusaders, thought that the Moslem Shrine was the actual temple of Solomon. Their church in London, set in the precinct of the Temple, (which was to be the home of the lawyers), was modelled on it, and so was the Round Church at Cambridge. Around the Dome of the Rock in Jerusalem Moslem religious colleges were ranged, and remain to this day.

The mild and tolerant rule of the Arabs, under which Jerusalem was a centre of culture of Moslems, Jews and Christians together, was rudely disturbed in the 10th century by the invasion of rougher Turkish tribes coming from Turkistan and Central Asia. Christian pilgrims were molested, and the Popes and Christian Princes in Europe proclaimed a Holy War to redeem the Shrines of Christendom from the hated Moslem occupation. So the 200 years war between west and east, which we know as the Crusades, was launched. For a time the Crusaders carried all before them, and established the Latin kingdom of Jerusalem on a feudal system. They brought a Western fanaticism. Unlike the Arab conquerors, they put all infidels to the sword, and the Jews were again excluded from the City. Their kingdom lasted less than a hundred years. At the fatal battle of Hattin (1187), on the hills above the Lake of Galilee, the flower of the Christian Knights was destroyed, and Saladin regained the holy city for the Crescent. Save for a short period in the 13th century from 1229, when the Holy Roman

Jerusalem

emperor, Frederick II, playing on the rivalries of the Emirs, secured by diplomacy the throne of Jerusalem, while allowing the Moslems to retain their holy place on the site of the Temple, the Crescent reigned supreme in Jerusalem till the World War 1914-1918.

Jerusalem, like the rest of Palestine, experienced for over a century the chaos caused by the invasion of the hordes of Mongols and Tartars. It was not till the Ottoman Turks in the 15th century spread their empire over the Middle East, and the Sultan Suliman, 'the Law-giver', restored the walls of the city (1541-2), that law and order were again assured, and the pilgrims of the three religious communities could make their way in security. The walls of Jerusalem, rebuilt by Suliman, have survived intact to the present day, save where a breach was made in 1898 to allow the German Emperor William II to drive into the portal of the Jaffa Gate. That was the year when Herzl, the founder of Zionism, came to Jerusalem to meet the Emperor.

Jews, driven out of Spain and Portugal by fanatical Christian monarchs at the end of the 15th century, turned to the benevolent, tolerant realm of the Turks; and Jewish schools again flourished in Jerusalem and in Galilee. The old city within the walls comprised Jewish, Christian and Moslem quarters. In the middle of the 19th century the population began slowly to spread over the hills and valleys without the walls. Jews multiplied their suburbs in the Western and Southern areas. Three principal synagogues were established in the old city: one of the Sephardim, which bore the revered name of Jochanan Ben Zaccai, who, after the destruction of Jerusalem and the Temple by the Romans, restored the schools, one of the Ashkanazim, called Hurva, (i.e. the destruction), one of the Hasidim, which was the place of worship of the mystics. The three were destroyed during the bitter struggle of the War of Independence in 1948.

A hundred years ago, Dean Stanley, a famous English divine and writer about Palestine, recorded that no permanent habitation was fixed outside the walls. Sir Moses Montefiore, who visited the Holy Land seven times between 1837 and his death in 1884, was the first to promote the building of Jewish residential quarters outside the walls. They bore his Hebrew name Moshe; Yemin Moshe, etc. A tribute to him, subscribed by Jews of many countries, was applied for the building of these quarters. Following this example, the Jewish bodies in Western Europe, which were concerned with the education and well-being of Jews in the city, built modern schools in the suburban quarters. The Christian churches likewise, and the many Orders of monks and nuns, emulating each other, multiplied their edifices in the suburbs. The Russians, who were the champions of the Orthodox Church, were first in the field, erecting vast hostels to house tens of thousands of Russian peasants who made the pilgrimage each year. Then the French, who were the champions of the Latin Church, built hostels, convents and orphanages. Later the Germans, who patronised both the Roman-Catholic and the Protestant Church, built four religious bastions around the city. The Italians built a hospital on the model of the Bargello of Florence. The English and the Scotch Christians were the most modest in their buildings; and of them it was said, when Great Britain became the ruling power in Palestine: 'The meek shall inherit the Earth.'

During the thirty years of the British Administration, 1918-1948, the area of Jerusalem was extended far beyond its borders in any previous age. It was the chief city of the Administration and the residence of the British High Commissioners, starting with Sir Herbert Samuel, 1920-5. It became also the centre of the Zionist movement and of the Jewish Agency for Palestine, which was the instrument of the Jews of the world for bringing back the people to the land of Israel and settling them on the soil. Jerusalem was also the seat of the Hebrew University, which arose on the splendid site of Scopus, the Hill of the Watchman, and part of the ridge of the Mount of Olives, where Titus was encamped when he destroyed the Temple. An archaeological museum worthy of the treasures of the past was

Jerusalem

built by the munificence of John Rockefeller, Junior, just outside the walls, by the gate named after Herod.

It is built, too, around a famous tree said to date from the time of the Crusaders. An old Arab tower was on the site, and had to go, but the tree remains. The building was carried out with loving care and without stinting of means. The walls are of that white glamorous stone with which Jerusalem is bountifully furnished. It is designed as an inn of tranquillity, detached from the hurly-burly of the modern city. The exhibition galleries surround a garden and a pool paved with blue tiles of a revived Jerusalem industry, and with reeds from Lake Huleh. The outer frieze of the galleries contains ten tablets, the work of the English sculptor Eric Gill, which mark the chief cultural influences of Palestine, Canaanite, Egyptian, Assyrian, Hebrew (represented by the Tables of Stone), Phoenician (by ships), Greek, Roman, Byzantine, Moslem and Crusader. England was not included, because her monuments were later than 1800 A.D.

The finds which are exhibited range from the earliest products of human art and craft, dating back to 20,000 B.C., to masterpieces of Egyptian, Hellenistic, Byzantine and Arab workmanship. They include the Galilee skull of primitive man, the skeletons of mesolithic man and woman from the caves of Athlit, models of houses dating to 5000 B.C., which were buried in the mound of Jericho, ritual objects of the Canaanite cults, Egyptian scarabs and jewellery from the era of the Pyramids, cuneiform tablets that are diplomatic correspondence of Egypt 1500-1400 B.C., the potsherd 'Letters of Lachish', written on earthenware in Biblical Hebrew, from the time of Jeremiah, sculptured sarcophagi of the Hellenistic age, and statues of Greek gods and goddesses, papyrus manuscripts of the Byzantine Empire, that were recovered from the ruined cities in Sinai; and lastly, hundreds of fragments of the Books of the Bible and the Apocrypha, 2000 years old, in Hebrew and in Greek, that were recovered in the latest years from the Dead Sea caves—but not the Seven Scrolls, which are in the Library of the

The New Old Land of Israel

Hebrew University. (See Chs. V, VIII, X.) Since 1947, the Museum sadly has been inaccessible to Jews.

When the Museum was built, Jew and Gentile worked together in archaeology, revealing the historic treasure of the Land, storing, arranging and interpreting it. During those thirty years of the British Mandate, schools and religious buildings of all the creeds were multiplied. Great, however, as was the expansion of Jerusalem in the period of the Mandate, the enlargement during the first ten years of the State of Israel has been beyond all that was done in the previous period. During the year of desperate struggle for independence, 1948, both Jewish and Arab Jerusalem suffered grievously from bombardment and shelling. The Jewish quarter within the walls, containing the three principal synagogues, was razed to the ground by the Arab armies after stout resistance of its inhabitants. Some Christian religious buildings which had been turned into fortresses were blown up. The Hebrew University and the Hadassah-University hospital by its side, though successfully defended against Arab attacks, were cut off from the Jewish town by an Arab strong-point. Despite provision in the Armistice agreement of 1949 between Israel and Jordan, that the Scopus area should be restored to its cultural purposes, and despite endless efforts of Israel to implement that Agreement, the position is unchanged. When the University was re-opened in 1949, it had to be accommodated for seven years in improvised buildings, dispersed over the hills and valleys on the west and south of the city. The buildings on Scopus remain a Jewish enclave, under protection of the United Nations, in the Arab area, and occupied by a small force of Jewish police.

During the first ten years of Israel a hundred thousand Jewish immigrants, out of the million who came to Israel, made their home in and around greater Jerusalem. The city has been proclaimed the Capital of the State, and government offices, some new, some transformed buildings of all kinds, have multiplied. A temporary Parliament House is in the main avenue built by the British administration and named after King George

Jerusalem

V. But a new civic and cultural centre, at once the Whitehall and the Bloomsbury of Jerusalem, is being built in an area known as Kirya—meaning City—which was an empty space to the south-west of the Jewish town, an undulating valley between two ridges. On one ridge the Government offices and the Parliament House, on the other the halls and laboratories of the Hebrew University, are rising at a magic pace, as though by a rub of Aladdin's lamp. The spacious and beautiful University buildings are designed for a student body that may reach 10,000. The Medical School and University hospital are rising on another commanding site, a high hill a few miles distant, beyond the former Christian village of Ein Karim, which is the traditional birth-place of John the Baptist. On the skyline of the new Jewish town three modern buildings stand out prominently by their size and height; and typify three diverse aspects of New Jerusalem; the convention centre, which is designed for Jewish and international congresses, and is built on the site of the camp of the Roman garrison of the 1st century—bricks marked with the stamp of the Tenth Legion were found—a Rabbinical centre, which is higher than any other institute, and a vast office building of the Labour Federation.

One of the happy changes in the landscape is the planting of trees, which in parts have become woodlands. The principal roads are tree-lined, and a green belt is planted on the hills around the new suburbs. Six million trees are to be a Memorial Forest for the six million Jews who were exterminated by the Nazis during the World War. The central memorial on the outskirts of the city is for the soldiers who fell in the War of Independence. Their graves are placed around the 'Hill of Herzl', whose body was brought from Vienna in the first year of the State to be re-interred. The Hill is a beauty spot of landscape gardening. If the new Jerusalem is not, in the Psalmist's words, 'built all compact together', it is, like the Old Jerusalem, 'beautiful in elevation'; and one day again it will be 'the joy of all the earth'. In the fullness of days it may be hoped that the three universal religions, Judaism, Christianity and Islam,

The New Old Land of Israel

which look to Jerusalem as the Holy City, will have there a visible symbol of their common faith in a single humanity.

III

The Coastal Plain: Jaffa and Caesarea

OF THE coastal towns of Israel from antiquity none is so famous as Jaffa. The Hebrew name means beautiful; and the former Arab city, rising in its terraces on a rounded promontory hill, straight from the sea and the rocky reefs that formed the ancient harbour, and surrounded by golden sands and orange groves and palms, deserved its name. Today Jaffa has lost some of her comeliness, because what was once an open garden area stretching to the north, and planted for miles with orange groves fragrant with blossom, has become a big, shapeless, crowded, modern city. That is Tel-Aviv, the biggest in Palestine and the cultural centre of Israel. A teeming suburb, also, now another town, on the southern side has occupied the sand-dunes. Since the establishment of the State of Israel, historic Jaffa and its greater off-spring Tel-Aviv—meaning Mound of Spring—have been combined in one Municipality, which administers a city of 350,000 inhabitants. Jaffa, however, still keeps the likeness of an ancient historic and oriental town, while Tel-Aviv, which did not exist before 1909, is proudly and undisguisedly new, modern, and Western.

Jaffa has since thirty years lost her pride of place as the principal port of Palestine. The rocky reefs, which run out from the promontory, gave shelter to the sailing-ships of old; but were an impediment to the entry of big steam-ships of today. In the first year of the British Mandate for Palestine, Jaffa was the place at which the immigrants landed; and

The New Old Land of Israel

oranges were shipped. But in 1921 it was the scene of serious Arab outbreaks against the Jews, and a large part of the Jewish population left. The British Administration were advised that the roadstead of Haifa, fifty miles to the North on the coast, protected as it was by the ridge of Carmel, could be turned to a good modern harbour. They carried out the work, and most immigrants and visitors in the Mandate time landed there. Jaffa and Tel-Aviv remained as minor roadsteads. Haifa, whose Hebrew name means haven, has become in the last ten years the naval and commercial port of the State of Israel, and one of the main harbours of the Eastern Mediterranean.

Like Jerusalem and other historic places in the land of Canaan, Jaffa (Yuppa), appears in the Egyptian monuments and documents some centuries before it came into the Hebrew Kingdom. It was conquered by several of the Pharaohs in the age—from the 17th to the 13th century B.C.—when they were contending with the Northern empires for the mastery of the East Mediterranean littoral. When Jaffa was lost to Egypt, it fell first into the hands not of the Hebrews, but of the Philistines, who in the 13th century B.C. came over the sea from the West—possibly from the Isle of Crete. It was not till David and Solomon extended their conquest over the whole of Canaan West of Jordan that it was an integral part of the Kingdom and the port of the King's navy: 'a gateway to the islands'. At Jaffa the Cedars of Lebanon, sent by King Hiram of Phoenician Tyre, for building the Temple of Jerusalem, were landed. They were floated on rafts from the Phoenician coast, and then carried—let us hope by wagon, but possibly by the three-score and ten thousand men whom the King chose to carry burdens—up the pass through the mountains of Judea. And when Zerubbabel rebuilt the Temple after the return from the Babylonian captivity, in accordance with the grant of Cyrus, King of Persia, he, too, brought the Cedars from Lebanon to the port at Jaffa.

The port, indeed, did not remain a permanent part of the Kingdom of Judah. After the golden era of King Solomon, the

The Coastal Plain: Jaffa and Caesarea

Philistines or the Phoenicians seem soon to have re-asserted their sway. The main outlet to the sea of the Kings of Judah was Etzion-Geber on the Gulf of Akaba (see p. 124). The Phoenicians were subdued in the 8th century B.C. by the Assyrian invaders from Nineveh in the north of Mesopotamia. Sennacherib, the Conqueror, records the capture of the city of Jaffa in a monument which, like the Lachish frieze (p. 77) is in the British Museum. Centuries later, after the defeat of the Persian King, the Macedonian conqueror Alexander the Great, who made himself master of the whole Syrian and Levant coast, turned Semitic Jaffa into Hellenistic Joppa, named after a Greek goddess, daughter of the god of the winds. And the Greek dynasty, the Ptolemies of Egypt, made it one of their ports.

We know today much more than our fathers about the past of Jaffa. Tel-Aviv, which began to rise from the sand-dunes in 1909, as a garden suburb, and spread with an amazing rapidity after the British Mandate was granted, lacked at first a credential of history. That reproach was removed in the Forties by archaeologists of the Hebrew University. Digging in one of several Tels, El Kassileh, near the mouth of the Yarkon river—known also by its Arab name, El Auja—which runs into the sea four miles north of Jaffa, they found sure evidence of an ancient trading city which had been occupied for 2,000 years. The Tel may cover the original Jaffa. It was certainly a place where maritime peoples met and exchanged their goods. Besides the walls and bases of towers, which are the common stock of archaeologists in the exploration of Palestine, the Tel gave up unmistakable records of several civilizations. The archaeologists traced 12 separate strata, each representing an era, and ranging from the Philistine occupation about 1300 B.C. to the Mameluke—Arab occupation and destruction about 1300 A.D. Each age has its own pottery, and there are indications here, as in other antiquity sites in Palestine, that copper was smelted. It was a principal article of commerce of the Phoenicians who mined it in Cyprus. The metal gave the name to the island. The water of the Yarkon River, which today supplies Jerusalem and the Negev by pipe-line, was then used for irrigation of the surrounding land, and so supported a considerable population. A sidelight on the standard of life was afforded by the finding of traces of a dye industry, and heaps of clay sinkers for keeping food hot.

The Philistine settlers had commercial relations with Phoenician cities to the north and with Egypt. A later Israel town was built on the ruins of the Philistine, and was destroyed, it seems, in 732 B.C., when the Assyrian Warrior King, Tiglath Pileser, he who took Israel captive, overran the coast. The diggers recovered from that era seals and scarabs and two pottery sherds inscribed with Hebrew cursive writing. They are judged to be of the 8th century, and concern royal property. The legend of one is: 'for the King, 1,000 . . . of oil'—the missing word being some measure—and the name of the officer. The other runs: 'gold of Ophir for Beth-Horon; shekels 30'—the number being represented by three parallel lines. Beth Horon, today a village above the Valley of Ajalon, which leads from the Coastal Plain to the Judean Plateau, was a strong depot of the King. Solomon built Beth-Horon, the upper and lower fenced cities with walls and gates (2 Chr. 8.5). Here at Tel Kassileh must have been one of his ports.

Of the Persian period a single building has been identified. But of pottery of that era there is abundance, including fragments of vases brought from Greece or Ionia, the western coast of Asia which was settled by the Greeks. One piece of the fifth century shows graceful dancers painted black on a red ground. From this period, too, is a Hebrew seal inscribed 'A servant of the King'. Nothing of moment was found in the Hellenistic and Roman layers; but in the Byzantine layer above them, and near the surface, many pottery fragments are stamped with the Cross of the Christian Church.

Tel Kassileh is not the only excavation of recent years to throw light on the early history of Jaffa. Working-men laying drainpipes for the ever-spreading Tel-Aviv are likely, without premeditation, to come across tombs and other relics of the

The Coastal Plain: Jaffa and Caesarea

buried past. Not seldom they are of the period of the Hyksos, who conquered Egypt from the North about 1700 B.C. The dynasty of Nomad chieftains of Central Asiatic origin held strongly the Palestine coast-road as part of the defence in depth of their empire. It was a strategic boulevard, and Jaffa was one of the fortress stations. One tomb, of the 17th or 16th century, gave up jewellery and scarabs, an ostrich egg, which then, as in more modern times, was esteemed an ornament, alabaster vases and daggers. In the tomb were ivory carvings, fashioned as the heads and manes of horses. The regard for the horse, the animal which had brought the Hyksos mastery in war, was a characteristic of the Dynasty. Near Kassileh another mound, Jerishe, was excavated, and revealed a Hyksos fortress with a sloping glacis, which was still intact. That confirmed the Hyksos occupation of the area.

We have a trustworthy picture of the houses in which the inhabitants of Jaffa lived five thousand years ago. A bulldozer, working outside Tel-Aviv, exposed a tomb containing ossuaries of pottery in the form of a house. In them were human bones, which made it clear that the practice of storing skeletons in a casket—common in the first centuries of the Christian era—has this ancient lineage. The house ossuaries are usually rectangular, sometimes standing on four pillars, and with a vaulted roof. A few, however, are round.

During the 1948 Arab-Jewish war, the evacuation by its Arab inhabitants of the Arab quarter, which was the major part of Jaffa, gave the opportunity for exploration of the core of the ancient town. Hitherto in Jaffa, as in Jerusalem, archaeological burrowing had been restricted. In 1956 a site above the port was excavated, and the lower levels, beneath the Byzantine, the Hellenistic, and Judaic, gave a rich vein. Part of the wall of the Canaanite town and the stone threshold of the town-gate, flanked by brick walls, and by its side the massive bronze hinge on which the wooden door swung, were uncovered. The lowest layer yielded a fragment of a stele (monumental tablet) with an inscription in Egyptian hieroglyphs, which was proved to date

The New Old Land of Israel

from the dynasty of Ramases (1400-1300 B.C.). The first name of Ramases II appears on one of the stone blocks of the wall.

Tel-Aviv is the one place in Israel in which the visitor is not conscious of history. It looks altogether modern. Yet there, too, history is buried a few feet beneath the ground. A cemetery of the early centuries of the Christian era was unearthed recently near the Russian Pilgrim Hostel of the Orthodox Church, which is in another suburb, and next to the University College of the town. The tombs contained hundreds of inscriptions, mainly Greek, but some Hebrew and Aramaic. One of the Greek marks the grave of the President of the community of Tarsus in Cilicia, the town of St. Paul's birth. Jaffa was in antiquity, as in the middle and modern ages, the favoured portal from overseas for Jerusalem. And the cemeteries of ancient Jaffa contain graves of Jews from afar who died on their journey or pilgrimage to the Holy City.

Another revealing find was a hoard of 850 coins, of the reign of the Maccabean conquering king of the 1st century B.C., Alexander Jannaeus (103-76 B.C.). They are all, too, of one type, called a star-anchor; on one side a star with a Hebrew legend, which is for the most part unintelligible, on the other an anchor with a Greek legend and the Greek name of the King. The Hebrew script of the coins is sometimes in the square letters that are used today in the scrolls of the Law read in the Synagogue. The interest of the find is rather in the naval and bilingual character of the pieces of money than in the wording of the legend. We know that the Maccabean princes made Jaffa one of the chief places of their kingdom, and built there a Jewish fleet which engaged in the Mediterranean trade. The Roman destruction in the second century B.C. of two maritime rival powers in the Mediterranean, Carthage and Corinth, left the seas open to Jewish enterprise. But not for long. The struggle in the first century A.D. of the Jews with Rome, which rent and ravaged the land of Israel, was waged on the sea as well as on the land. From that age Roman coins found in Jaffa bear the effigy of Titus and the legend—Judaea Navalis or

The Coastal Plain: Jaffa and Caesarea

Victor Navalis—to commemorate a Roman naval victory which was fought at Jaffa.

For Christians, as for Jews, Jaffa has religious associations. One of the first women to accept the Gospel of Jesus was Tabitha, or Dorcas, of Jaffa, 'a woman full of good works', whom the apostle Peter visited. She has given her name to endless societies of good workers; and an annual feast in her memory is celebrated by the Christians of Jaffa. Peter stayed in the house of Simon the Tanner; and tradition has not neglected the opportunity of creating a holy place to be visited by pilgrims. The house, which in modern times has played that role, has no pretence of Antiquity; but the reputed visit of Peter has assured the devotion of the various Christian churches through the ages. And European pilgrims of the Middle Ages were lodged in vaults known as St. Peter's Cellars. The association of the Holy Place made Jaffa a town of special concern for the Crusaders in the two centuries of struggle between the Cross and the Crescent. King Richard Coeur-de-Lion of England fought Saladin outside the walls and defeated him. The medieval town and its walls were finally razed to the ground by the Mameluke Sultan Baibars (c.1290), who made it his aim to destroy utterly every Christian base on the coast, so that any fresh Crusade should find no foothold.

In the age of discovery, some centuries later, the orange, which has brought fame to Jaffa, was taken there by Portuguese mariners, and found its best soil in gardens in the Plain of Sharon. In the Arab countries it has kept till the present day the name Burtukan, meaning the Portuguese fruit: (Arabic B is regularly substituted for P). Jaffa became again a port of more than local significance in the 19th century, after Napoleon Bonaparte marched from Egypt up the coast; and thirty years later Ibrahim Pasha, moving from Egypt, occupied Palestine and a large part of Syria. Jerusalem and the Holy Land began to attract the attention not only of Pilgrims but of Governments. The 'Eastern Question' was a constant international issue. Jaffa was the seat of European Consuls and Vice-Consuls;

The New Old Land of Israel

and the early organizations for European settlement in the Holy Land there fixed their first homes. Sir Moses Montefiore, the Anglo-Jewish philanthropist of the Victorian Age, the Christian German 'Templars', and the Jewish 'Lovers of Zion' planted agricultural 'Colonies' in the neighbourhood. The first Jewish agricultural College, supported by the French body Alliance Israelite Universelle, and named Mikveh Israel—the gathering of Israel—was opened more than eighty years ago in the outskirts of the town. And the first Hebrew Secondary School, the 'Gymnasia' as it was called, was established in Jaffa. Strange that the word, which signified a Greek abomination for the Maccabees, signifies today the Hebrew revival.

A new destiny for the town started almost casually by the building of a small garden-city for Jewish residents. Tel-Aviv was at first, and remained till the end of the first world war, one of the several modern middle-class suburbs. Violent clashes in the old port of Jaffa between Arabs and Jews in 1921 gave a great impetus to the extension of the quarter into a township which should be all-Jewish and controlled by Jews. The idea of local autonomy was enthusiastically taken up by one of the founders of the garden-city and its first Mayor, Meir Dizengoff. Further outbreaks of trouble between Jews and Arabs, in 1929 and 1936, particularly affected the mixed population of Jaffa, and were made the opportunity of shifting the Jewish population and severing the municipal links with the older city. And the big —for the Mandate period relatively big—immigration of the first years of the Hitler persecution, 1933-1936, brought Tel-Aviv a large increase of population, and particularly of the cultural talents. While Jerusalem was the British Administration capital, the all-Jewish township was the political, social and artistic centre of Palestine Jewry (Yishuv). The Palestine Symphony Orchestra (now the Israel Philharmonic), created in the Thirties by the enthusiasm of Hubermann, the famous violinist, from the exiled Jewish musicians of Europe, had and has its home in Tel-Aviv. So had, and has, the dramatic company hailing originally from Russia, the Habima, which has become the

The Coastal Plain: Jaffa and Caesarea

national theatre. So has the powerful, comprehensive Labour organization, the Histadrut, which comprises all the trade unions, the co-operative producer and consumer societies, the agricultural Collectives, and vast contracting and transport enterprises. So have most of the Hebrew daily, weekly and monthly journals. And the triennial gathering of young Jews and Jewesses from all parts of the world for athletic games, the Maccabead, takes place in Tel-Aviv and one of its satellite towns, Ramat Gan (Garden Hill).

Before the end of the British Mandate for Palestine, Tel-Aviv—without Jaffa—was far the largest city of Palestine and the most modern. It had long surpassed Jaffa in numbers, wealth and influence; in the strained political period, from 1945, it was the pivot of Jewish activity. After the decision of the United Nations in November 1947, about the partition of Palestine, the population of Jaffa and Tel-Aviv waged a kind of civil war till, shortly before the Mandate ended, Jaffa fell into Jewish hands, and most of its Arab population fled and did not return. The Israel Declaration of Independence was read and signed on May 14th, 1948, in the Art Museum of Tel-Aviv. The seat of Government and of the elected Assembly of Israel, the Knesset, and the Ministries were in Tel-Aviv till 1950. The Ministries were housed in what had been the Christian German village Sarona—named after Sharon—two miles to the north, which had been finally engulfed by the Jewish town. Jerusalem has been, since 1950, the capital of Israel, as history and Jewish feeling required. But the new-old Tel-Aviv—Jaffa remains a cultural hearth of the Hebrew renaissance. And the Israel Labour organization—Histadrut—has there a huge central office, commonly called the Kremlin.

The emergence of Tel-Aviv as the biggest city of the country in the twentieth century recalls the emergence of another port-town in the first century B.C. Caesarea Ad Mare (on sea) was built with great magnificence in the Greek style by Herod the Great, in honour of his patron Augustus Caesar; and its port was called Sebastos, which is the Greek rendering of the

The New Old Land of Israel

Emperor's first name. It became in a short time the most important town and harbour of the Roman province of Palestine. It had in its heyday a mixed population of a quarter of a million. Herod built it around the site of a small Phoenician harbour, which was called Strato's Tower, from the name of a king of Sidon. The Phoenicians ruled over this section of the coast in the Persian period. Herod conceived the idea of building a great town to serve as a stronghold of Roman naval power on the Mediterranean coast between the ports of Syria and Egypt. Josephus tells how all the streets led in radial directions to the harbour, and were intersected by parallel avenues. 'What was the greatest and most laborious work of all was the haven that was always free from the waves. Its size was not less than the Piraeus; and there was a double section for the ships . . . There were also many arches where the sailors dwelt and a large quay . . . Over against the mount of the haven upon a hill there was a temple of Caesar.' From a vast hippodrome, also built by Herod, there remain four obelisks and the debris of arches and colonnades.

It was at Caesarea that Pontius Pilate had his palace, and that St. Paul was brought before the Roman Governor Felix. It was there, too, that bitter fighting broke out between the Jews and Gentiles in 66 A.D., and touched off the Jewish war against the Romans. In the second century a new Jewish community grew up and flourished. The famous Rabbi Akiva, who was the spiritual leader of the Revolt of Bar-Cochba against Hadrian, 135 A.D., was put to death at Caesarea. Its rabbinical schools and its Christian schools were equally famous in the 3rd and 4th centuries. Another celebrated Rabbi, Abbahu, was the head of the Talmudic college, and a splendid synagogue of his period has been recently unearthed close to the Sea. It was built over the foundation of a building in the Herodian style, which may have belonged to the original city. The names of the benefactors inscribed on the walls are Greek, and the inscriptions are in Greek. A Corinthian capital of the Synagogue bore the decoration of the menorah, a symbol of the mingling of Jewish

The Coastal Plain: Jaffa and Caesarea

and Greek culture. The Greek language remained dominant.

Two of the Christian worthies of Caesarea, Origen A.D. 185-254, and Eusebius (c.300) were among the most eminent religious philosophers and historians of the early Church. Recent excavations have exposed the mosaic floor of a Christian church with life-like pictures of all the wild animals, including an elephant and hippopotamus. They have restored, too, many monuments of the ancient splendour of the Roman town, some recovered from the bottom of the sea, some from the sands which submerged the Roman theatres, forums, temples, and aqueducts. Two colossal statues of emperors, one of porphyry and one of white marble, but both headless, now adorn the Byzantine forum, built by a mayor who recorded his name. The ruins of the amphitheatre show that it was bigger than the Colosseum of Rome itself. Caesarea remained the capital of Palestine in the Byzantine Empire; and it was a great bishopric of the Christian Church, second only to Jerusalem. It corresponded with Canterbury in Saxon Britain.

Caesarea retained some importance through the Middle Ages as a port. It was a Crusader stronghold; and Louis IX of France, who led one of the later Crusades in 1251, when the Latin Kingdom of Jerusalem was breaking up, made it his headquarters. He built a castle of which the foundations survive. And the medieval city walls rise from the fallen Roman monuments. But the Christian possession was short-lived. The same ruthless Mameluke Sultan, Baibars, who destroyed the walls of Jaffa, Askalon and Acre, destroyed the citadel of Caesarea. And so completely did he ravage the countryside for miles around that what had been a Paradise, a fertile region of orchards and gardens, was turned into a desolate swamp infested with malaria and deserted by man and beast.

It was not till the latter part of the 19th century that a settled population returned. At first the ruins were occupied by a group of Moslem Bosnians, who had taken refuge in Turkey when their country was annexed to the Austro-Hungarian Empire. The Jews came only as settlers on the land after

The New Old Land of Israel

the British Mandatory Administration was established. A clause of the Mandate directed the administration 'to encourage, in co-operation with the Jewish Agency for Palestine, the close settlement of Jews on the land, including waste-lands not required for public purposes'. The Palestine Jewish Colonization Association, founded by Baron Edmond de Rothschild, the Sire of the Jewish Return to the soil of the land of the Bible, obtained from the Government of Palestine a lease of the wasteland and the sand-dunes and swamps around Caesarea. They set about to restore the man-made desert by man's science to its old fertility, and rapidly brought about a transformation.

In the last period of the Mandate, when the Jewish population was striving to bring into the country survivors of the Nazi concentration camps in Europe, who had not been able to get immigration certificates from the British Government, the region of Caesarea was a favourite place for running the blockade of the coast. It served also as a place of gun-running by both Jews and Arabs. Fierce fighting took place on the shore in the War of Independence, and the Jews prevailed. Today the Arab inhabitants have left, and the old town within the medieval walls is shattered and deserted. The area round it, on the other hand, is occupied by thriving Jewish villages. Amid the ruins of Caesarea itself Jewish agricultural settlers and a fishing group have planted a modern village with the name of S'dot Yam (sea meadows). And they have built a museum to house the antiquity finds of amateurs which are multiplied, and named it after a heroic woman settler, Hannah Senesh, from Hungary. She volunteered in the World War for service with the British Forces, and was dropped by parachute in her native land to organize the resistance against the Nazis. She was taken and executed, dying bravely. She wrote poems while in the Kibbutz, and one of her lines has become a household word in Israel. 'Blessed be the match that kindles the flame and is consumed.'

It was one of the last enterprises of Baron James de Rothschild, the son cf Baron Edmond, to lay out a golf links in the

4. An aerial view of Jaffa. In the foreground the garden of the Russian church where the Jewish Necropolis was found.

Jaffa and Tel-Aviv, Israel

5. Roman Emperor's statue

Right: Askalon, Greco-Roman statue and columns

6. The white tower of the Mosque at Ramleh

7. *Above:* Model of King Solomon's stable at Megiddo

Left: Beth Alpha. Mosaic of synagogue

Right: Capital from Caesarea with Jewish candelabra and Greek ornament

The Coastal Plain: Jaffa and Caesarea

sand-dunes around Caesarea. Nature has fitted the place for that sport, as much as in Roman days it was fitted for a vast Hippodrome. The golfer of the future, hitting his ball out of a bunker, may perhaps enjoy the excitement of uncovering Roman coins and other relics of the past.

In the heart of the hill in the ridge of Carmel, which overlooks the Coastal Plain around Caesarea teeming with fresh life, the body of Baron Edmond, at his testamentary request, has been laid to rest. His spirit dominates the region. For it was his vision which turned a malarial swamp into a smiling landscape. And the young Jewry he helped is conscious that the rebirth of the living people is linked with the resurrection of the past.

IV

The Judean Foothills: Gezer and Modiin

THE Judean foothills, known in Hebrew as the Shefela, that is, the Lowlands, were a cradle of Hebrew Prophets. They were, too, the scene of the heroic struggle of the Maccabees against the Hellenistic Greek Armies over two thousand years ago, and in our day they were the testing ground for the Army of Israel in the War of Independence 1948. The decisive campaign was the Battle of the Road, that winds through these foothills from the coast to Jerusalem. It was fought, during the last six months of the British Mandate—December 1947 to May 1948—and the first two months of the State of Israel, by the Jewish volunteer army (Hagana) in order to raise the siege of Jewish Jerusalem. The city was attacked and beleaguered by Arab armies from three sides, south, north and east. Only on the west side, and by heroic efforts, could Jewish forces, based on a few agricultural villages in the foothills, keep the way open for the food convoys which must sustain the 100,000 Jewish inhabitants of the city. History has proved through the ages that the command of a few strong places in the foothills, guarding the road from the plain to the plateau, was the target of the invaders and the strength of the defenders.

The story of Gezer, a fortress-town often mentioned in the Bible, illustrates the lesson. It is not to be confused with Gaza of the Philistines, though it is not far from it, and was also like Gaza a Philistine stronghold. The Mound of Gezer was excavated 1902-1909, before the first World War, by Professor

The Judean Foothills: Gezer and Modiin

Macalister, for the Palestine Exploration Fund, and was among the first sites to be explored scientifically. It turned out to cover the history of Man's progress for 5,000 years, from cave dwellings in the Stone Age to a Crusader's Castle. In the Middle Ages it suddenly disappeared from notice and habitation; and it was reoccupied by permanent settlers only in this century.

In the latter years of the nineteenth century the French Archaeologist-Consul, M. Clermont-Ganneau, he who found the inscribed stone in King Hezekiah's Water Tunnel in Jerusalem, was searching for Gezer, and read in an Arab history of the Middle Ages an account of a Bedouin raid in the Plain of Sharon. The raiders were pursued to the 'Mound of Jezar', between Ramleh and Hulda. He conjectured that Jezar might be Gezer, because its situation in the foothills of Judea fitted. His conjecture was confirmed a year later when, by a remarkable stroke of fortune, he found, within a mile of the mound, an inscription on a stone with the Hebrew words: 'Boundary of Gezer' on one side, and a Greek name on the other. It was of the period of the Maccabees. Some years later Professor Macalister started his systematic digging of the mound for the Palestine Exploration Fund, and carried it on for ten years. In those days the archaeologists in the Holy Land sank a shaft deep down in the mound, and started their digging at the bottom levels. There he discovered habitations of cave-dwelling troglodytes and a subterranean water tunnel like that in Jerusalem. The entrance was 23 feet high, and a rock-hewn staircase of eighty steps led to a spring a hundred feet below the surface. The tunnel must have been made by the Canaanites, or their predecessors, for securing water, in case of siege, from the spring deep down in the limestone. The early population, like the builders of Jericho, showed remarkable skill and purposefulness in their building. (See p. 131).

Macalister found at higher levels traces of animal and human sacrifice, and a High Place of seven erect stones, five to ten feet high, which must have been the centre of worship, something similar to the English Stonehenge, on a tiny scale. In these

The New Old Land of Israel

levels also he found many scarabs and other relics of Egyptian occupation. One of the scarabs was of the Pharaoh Amenhotep of the 15th century B.C., who is believed by some scholars to be the Pharaoh of the Exodus.

The earliest written record of Gezer is not in the Hebrew Bible, but in the cuneiform tablets of El Amarna (see p. 33), written from Canaan to the Pharoah's foreign office, when the Egyptian dominion over Syria and Palestine was threatened in the 14th century B.C. The Lord of Gezer writes to his overlord in Egypt, as Abd-Khiba wrote from Jerusalem (see page 34), complaining of the hostile Habiri. A century later Gezer appears on the famous monument of Merenptah, a later Pharaoh, boasting of his reconquest of the Land of Canaan: 'Gezer is seized; Israel is without seed'. An ivory sundial with a cartouche of that Pharaoh was found in Gezer. The town is mentioned several times in the Bible story of the Hebrew conquest of Canaan. Joshua smote the King of Gezer who came to help the King of Lachish. (Jos.10.33). 'The children of Ephraim thrust not out the Canaanites that dwelt in Gezer'. (*ib*.16.10). And again in the book of Judges: (1.29) 'The Canaanites dwelt among the Ephraimites in Gezer and became tributaries'. In the Book of Kings (1.9.16) it is written: 'Pharaoh, King of Egypt, went up to take Gezer and burnt it with fire. He slew the Canaanites that dwelt in the city, and gave it for a present unto his daughter, King Solomon's wife. And Solomon rebuilt Gezer.' The gate of Solomon's city has been identified; it corresponds exactly with that unearthed at Hazor. (See p. 107).

The fortress then constantly changed hands in the struggle between the Egyptians and the Canaanites, the Philistines and the Hebrews. It did not permanently remain in the Kingdom of Judah. Laying in the line of march of the armies of the Great Powers, it fell when the Assyrians invaded Judah in the reign of Manasseh the Wicked (2 Chr. 33.11). From that period we have burnt clay tablets in the Assyrian or Aramaic language that record legal contracts. The most exciting of the documents of this period of the Kingdom of Judah, however, is a tablet in

The Judean Foothills: Gezer and Modiin

Phoenician-Hebrew script, ascribed to the 10th century B.C. It gives a description of the calendar, which must have been made for cultivators of the soil: 'month of ingathering, month of sewing, month of pulling up the flax'. That is one of the earliest examples of connected Hebrew writing which has come down to us; and taken together with the clay tablets in Aramaic, which date from the same period, it is evidence that two languages were in use simultaneously in a city of mixed population.

Twenty-five years after Macalister finished his investigations a second and minor dig was carried out by the Australian archaeologist, Alan Rowe, in another section of the mound. It yielded nothing very spectacular, but a limestone altar with a sculpted reproduction of sacred trees, a part of the Canaanite cult, and tombs of the 11th century B.C., containing among the objects an agate figure of a cat sacred to an Egyptian goddess. At a lower level of the tomb chamber there was pottery a thousand years older. More sensational was the chance find of an inscribed potsherd among the debris from the Tel. It gave another early example of Semitic writing, more ancient than the Phoenician Hebrew. The script was semi-pictorial, semi-alphabetic, called the Sinai script, because specimens of it were found in the area where the Children of Israel wandered after the Exodus.

The evidence unearthed by the archaeologists points to the maintenance of pagan worship in the period of the Kingdom of Judah. Astarte (in Hebrew Ashtoreth) was the favourite idol. Other places on the coastal plain of Palestine which have been excavated tell the same story. At Naharia, now a seaside resort in Western Galilee, ten miles north of Acre, and planned by Jewish refugees from Germany, a small mound within a few yards of the shore was excavated by local archaeologists. The Tel of only half an acre in area gave a vivid record of Canaanite worship. First the diggers found a square building erected on virgin soil, and dating before 2,000 B.C. Outside it was a small 'high place', a circle of big stones. Later a larger temple was

The New Old Land of Israel

built by the side of the other. The altar was there, and a box of metal figurines of a goddess, in silver and bronze. She is identified with Ashera, a sea-goddess who appears often in the Ugarit texts. One figurine is of a half-naked body, in which the breasts and navel are prominent. The head is crowned by a high tiara, and round the neck are rows of beads of semi-precious stones. Another wears a light conical hat; and two pointed horns protrude from under it. The stone mould from which the figurines were cast was on the spot. So, too, were a number of bowls with seven cups, perhaps for incense. They were apparently votive offerings; and seven was for the Canaanite, as for the Hebrews, a sacred number. Round the 'high place' also were masses of bones of animals, which must have been offered for sacrifice. The figurines of the goddess may have been offerings by the worshippers, or souvenirs which they could buy. Similar figurines and seven-cupped bowls were found in the temple area of Gezer and Megiddo, and at Byblos on the Phoenician coast, and more recently at Herzlia near Jaffa. Ashera and Ashtoreth were the principal Phoenician and Canaanite deities.

After the return of the Jews from the Babylonian captivity Gezer was again a place of mixed population. As we have noted, the inscribed stone which Clermont-Ganneau found in his search for the site had on one side a Greek name and on the other Hebrew words. From the evidence of antiquity we can picture two tribal groups within the small walled city, each living in its own quarter and having its own worship. In the days of the Kingdom of Judah they were Hebrew and Canaanite; in the period after the Babylonian Exile, they were Persians and Jews, and later, Greeks and Jews. Gezer renewed its importance in Jewish history during the struggle between the Maccabees and the Hellenists. It was a strong point again in the defence of the road from the coast to Jerusalem. The Book of the Maccabees tells that it was captured by Simon, the youngest brother of Judas, and that he made his residence there. A signal confirmation of that story came to light in the

The Judean Foothills: Gezer and Modiin

excavation. A fragment of a Greek tablet bore the words: 'may fire pursue Simon's palace', and the name Pampras. Professor Macalister recognized that the tablet was a magic imprecation designed to wreak vengeance, such as was common in Egypt and Palestine from the second millennium B.C. The first written mention of Jerusalem which has come to us, and of Hazor, occurs on such a tablet. Remarkably the belief in this form of magic, by which the tablet was broken and thereby the power of the enemy named would be broken, survived 1500 years. Pampras may have been the Greek commander, or one of his officers, in the fortress which Simon had captured.

At Gezer—Gazara in its Greek form—the Jews and the Greeks, and Judaism and Hellenistic religions were mixed, just as the Canaanite and the Hebrew peoples and religions had earlier co-existed side by side. The objects found in the Hellenistic layer included an altar with an inscription on either side, in Hebrew, 'to Jehovah', and a Greek dedication to the God Heracles. That is typical of the religious contamination against which the Maccabees fought their struggle.

Gezer does not come into the story of the Jewish struggle against the Romans. No relics of the Roman or Talmudic period were discovered in the Tel. It is not till the age of the Crusaders, more than 1000 years after the Maccabees bore rule, that it enters history once more. Then it is a fortress with its biblical name disguised as Gisard. Saladin camped there when he was negotiating peace with Richard Coeur-de-Lion, the King of England. In the prolonged period of confusion, that followed the expulsion of the Crusaders, when Mongols, Tartars and Turkomans invaded and ravaged the Land, the fortress and its name disappeared from memory.

The revival of Gezer as the home of a community in modern days followed the revelation of its historic past at the beginning of the century. The site was acquired for Jewish settlement by Baron Edmond de Rothschild, who laid the foundation of the Jewish home in Palestine. In 1913 he transferred the cultivable land, about 1000 acres—but without the historic Tel

The New Old Land of Israel

which had been excavated—to an English Zionist enterprise that bore the name of the heroic Maccabee family. The Maccabean Land Company was established shortly before the First World War, and before the Balfour Declaration; and had as its aim to help English Jews to settle as pioneers on the soil. The writer's father was the creator of the company. In 1923, Sir Herbert Samuel, then the High Commissioner, inaugurated the first Anglo-Jewish agricultural 'Colony' in Palestine; and the hopes were high that 100 families would settle. The hopes were not fulfilled in the next twenty years, because of the failure to find sufficient subterranean water. The land was tranferred by the Company during the World War to the Jewish National Fund, the instrument of the Zionist Organization for acquiring land as a Trust and settling Jews upon it. The Fund had more resources than the Company; and water was found. During the war, when food production was urgent, it contrived to place on the site a group of young people, some English, but mostly from Central Europe, who had received their agricultural preparation in a children's village conducted by the Hadassah Women's Organization of America. The name Hadassah was added to Gezer, and has remained.

The settlement flourished; and in the Israel War of Independence Gezer-Hadassah was a strong point guarding the road between the sea and Jerusalem. Fierce fighting was waged in the foothills around it, and the settlement itself was attacked and suffered grave damage. It was held against the Arab onslaught, and remained in the territory of Israel, in the corridor from the foothills to Jerusalem, right on the frontier. A vital part of the Jerusalem-Tel-Aviv highway which passed close to the mound was, however, in Arab hands; and the Jews had to build a new road to Ramleh. They called it the Road of Courage, and Gezer is one of the semi-military 'colonies' that guard it.

A few miles from the old highway on the other side, in the foothills to the North, and close to the Vale of Ajalon, where Joshua gained a great victory over the Canaanites while the

The Judean Foothills: Gezer and Modiin

sun stood still, another historic place is identified. The village of Modiin is the traditional birthplace, home and burial-place, of the Maccabee family. It is not mentioned in the Hebrew Bible, but only in the Books of the Maccabees. By a curious fate the story of the heroic exploits of Mattathias and his sons was excluded from the Holy Canon, while the less heroic and less noble story of Esther and Mordecai was included. The reason is probably that the heads of the Pharisee Schools, in whom the decision about the Canon lay, were involved in a bitter conflict with the Maccabee ruling house and the degenerate priest-kings of the 1st century B.C., when the Canon was fixed. Be this as it may, Modiin was a place of pilgrimage in the Middle Ages for both Jews and Christians. The tomb of the Maccabee brothers erected by Simon was a landmark. Of that tomb it is said in the Book of the Maccabees: 'And Simon built the monument upon the sepulchre of his father and his brothers, and raised it aloft with polished stone. And he set up seven pyramids, one over against the other, for his father and his mother and his brethren. And upon the pillars he fashioned all manner of arms for a perpetual memory, and besides the arms ships were carved that they should be seen of all that sail on the sea.' The Jews of that militant age, like those of today, aspired to be a maritime nation.

The monument of the Maccabees at Modiin is mentioned in the pilgrims' chronicles till the 14th century. It is shown on a famous mosaic map of Palestine of the 6th century, which was found on the floor of a church at Madeba across Jordan. (See Ch. 2 p. 45). The Christian pilgrims of the Middle Ages describe it. One of the last who set out from England, Sir John Mandeville, writing in 1356, says: 'Pilgrims go from Ramleh to Mount Modiin; and there lies the Prophet Maccabeus'.

Thereafter the record of the place and the monument is lost till the second half of the 19th century. In the era of invasion by Mongols and Tartars of the Holy Land during the fourteenth and following centuries, many ancient monuments were removed, and the identity of the Bible sites was lost. But in 1870

The New Old Land of Israel

the Palestine Exploration Fund of England carried out a survey of an Arab village called El Madyeh. There were caves known as 'Kubur El Yahud' (Tombs of the Jews); and these early archaeologists thought they were the remnants of the Maccabean sepulchre. Lord—then Lt.—Kitchener, some years later, made a more thorough examination of the region, and reported that the 'Tombs of the Jews' were not the graves of the Maccabees. But above the village a round hill with a rock-hewn sepulchre, which had been turned to a cistern, caught his attention. A Mohammedan Holy Place occupied the top of the hill. 'I have no doubt,' wrote Kitchener 'that this was the site of the tombs of those celebrated heroes of later Jewish history. The hill appears to me to fulfil all the requisites of this important and disputed site.'

In 1897, a few months before the holding of the first Zionist Congress, my father conducted to Palestine the 'Maccabean Pilgrimage' from England. It was organized through the Maccabean Society, and the pilgrims included the writer Israel Zangwill. My father met in Jerusalem an American Christian, a religious enthusiast, who had bought the lands of the Arab village, and was willing to sell. The Anglo-Jewish Society of the Maccabeans made an offer for the purchase of the tombs and the surrounding land; but it was rejected, and the village remained in Arab hands. Near it, however, a Jewish settlement has been established for fifty years, and has played a significant part in the National Home. It began with the acquisition of an area for planting a forest to commemorate Herzl, the creator of the Zionist Movement. One of the earliest industrial enterprises of the Jewish return was an olive-oil factory adjoining the forest, and named Ben Shemen, i.e. the place of oil. Then a home for orphaned Jewish children from Russia, whose parents were killed in the anti-Jewish pogroms of 1903 and 1905, was placed there. After the first World War in 1927 that home and a large area of land were taken for a kindred purpose, the training for agricultural life of war-orphans from Eastern Europe and Jewish youth of Palestine.

The Judean Foothills: Gezer and Modiin

Ben Shemen, under the direction of a German children's-doctor, an educator of genius, became a model children's village and attracted boys and girls of the country, as well as from Europe, by its combination of the humanities and agricultural education and its free spirit. When Hitler's persecution of Jews menaced all the young German-Jewish generations, it was to Ben Shemen that the first groups turned for the preparation for the new life. The children's village grew to a community of some hundreds of young persons, and it has remained that for thirty years.

The guiding aim of Ben Shemen was to train the young from childhood for life in the village, and to build up the sense of community and mutual responsibility. It played a decisive part in the movement of Children and Youth Immigration—Aliya, the Hebrew word, means spiritual as well as physical going up. Starting in 1933 to rescue German-Jewish youth, the movement grew rapidly during the World War to be the instrument for saving homeless Jewish boys and girls from all countries. Ben Shemen, during that period, has received ten thousand children and youth: and a large majority of them have remained loyal to the ideal of cultivating the land. Many have become youth leaders and teachers in other village communities. Thousands are pioneers of frontier settlements in Israel. In the period of bitter fighting in the War of Independence the young people of Ben Shemen, which was a border village on the frontier with Jordan, had to be evacuated. The children returned in 1951, and the good-neighbourly relations with Arabs, which the Director had fostered, were not severed.

Lydda (in Hebrew, Lod) is a town in the plain, a few miles from Ben Shemen. It is mentioned in the Bible in the Book of Chronicles, which tells that, after the return from the Babylonian Captivity, the men of the tribe of Benjamin built Lod (I Chr. 8,12). After the destruction of the Temple by the Romans, it was a famous seat of Rabbinical schools. It became a Roman colony with the name Diospolis about the end of the 2nd century A.D. Traditionally it was the home of one of the early Christian martyrs, St. George, who became the patron saint of England. The cathedral of the Orthodox Church, dating from the Middle Ages, bears his name. Today most of the inhabitants are Jews. But a few Christians and a few Moslem Arabs remain. The main airfield of Israel is situate close to the town and bears the Hebrew name Lod.

The village of Modiin, hitherto occupied by Arabs, fell into Jewish hands during the ten days of open war in July 1948. The Maccabean festival, which is among the most popular of national holidays, is now directly associated each year with the home of the Maccabees. Tradition links it with the eight-branch candelabra—adopted in our day as the coat-of-arms of Israel—because of the miracle by which a cruse of oil found in the temple of Jerusalem when Judah drove out the Hellenisers, and removed their abominations, lasted for eight days to feed the perpetual light. Today Israel youths on the first eve of the festival run from Modiin to Jerusalem and Tel-Aviv, carrying torches for lighting the big Menorahs in the towns. The opening also of the Maccabean athletic festival, which is held in Israel every few years, and brings together athlete teams from the four corners of Jewry, is marked by the lighting of the Flame of the Games with a burning torch brought by runners from Modiin to the Stadium. Modiin is a symbol of the heroic spirit by which Jews won their independence two thousand one hundred years ago, and won it again in our day.

V

The Philistine Coast: Lachish and Askalon

————————————————

AT THE exhibition of the Land of the Bible held in the British Museum in 1954, many of the most striking objects came from a place in ancient Judea, Lachish, which hitherto was little known except to professional students of the Bible and archaeology. The place is mentioned often in the historical books, Joshua and Judges, Kings and Chronicles. It is mentioned also in the Books of Isaiah and Jeremiah. But the site was lost. Lachish was a strongpoint in the defence of the Kingdom of Judah. It was situated in the foothills, between the coast and the mountain plateau on which Jerusalem stood. It is vividly portrayed in a famous Assyrian monument, which is a treasure of the British Museum. A bas-relief shows the Assyrian Army laying siege to it, the spearmen with their crested helmets, the slingers and the bowmen, and below them the chiefs of the town humiliated before the conquerors. The monument depicted the siege and capture of the fortress by Sennacherib in the 8th century B.C. Besides the relief, an eight-sided prism in the Museum recorded in cuneiform script Sennacherib's account of his exploits when he invaded King Hezekiah's kingdom. The remark that he had locked up the king, 'like a bird in a cage' (see page 37) occurs in that story.

The Book of Isaiah tells the dramatic story of the capture of the fortress city by Sennacherib, the Assyrian conqueror of whom Byron wrote:

The New Old Land of Israel

'The Assyrian came down like a wolf on the fold.
And his cohorts were gleaming with silver and gold.'

It was from Lachish that he sent a great army to Jerusalem against King Hezekiah (Isaiah 36.2). The head of the host, Rab-Shakeh, said to the emissaries of Hezekiah: 'Thus saith the great King, the King of Assyria. What confidence is this wherein thou trusteth, in the staff of the broken reed . . . on Egypt, whereon if a man leans, it will go into his hand and pierce it.' Lachish had fallen: but Jerusalem did not fall, because the Angel of the Lord went forth and smote the Assyrian host in their camp. And Lachish was again a fortress of Judah till the Babylonian invasion under Nebuchadnezzar. Then it was again destroyed (587 B.C.), and this time Jerusalem and the Temple were taken and destroyed, and the King and people of Judah went into Captivity.

Sixty years ago the father of modern biblical archaeology, Sir Flinders Petrie, directed the excavation of a big mound in the foothills of Judea, believing that he would find the historical Lachish beneath the piled-up debris. He thought indeed that he had succeeded. The place had not been rebuilt after the Babylonian destruction, and so all the evidence was of the biblical period. The layers of the mound gave proof of continuous Canaanite and Hebrew occupation. And a precious clay tablet which was discovered bore a cuneiform inscription with the name of a man mentioned in the Egyptian royal archives of Amarna as governor of Lachish. Flinders Petrie's identification, however, was questioned; and thirty years later one of his disciples, the late Mr. Starkey—who was killed by Arabs during the Palestine troubles in 1937—led an expedition to another Tel nearby. This mound bore the name of Duweir, meaning the little Convent. After three years digging, Starkey had positive proof that he had struck the Biblical site of Lachish which he was seeking.

More than that, he recovered sensational documents of history: a number of pottery sherds which were inscribed in Hebrew writing. When deciphered by a Professor of the He-

The Philistine Coast: Lachish and Askalon

brew University of Jerusalem, they turned out to be letters or reports written in the time of the Prophet Jeremiah, during Nebuchadnezzar's invasion of the kingdom. They were addressed by an officer commanding an outpost to the Commander of the army of Judah in Lachish. The name Lachish appears not only in one of the dispatches, but also inscribed on a boundary stone. The name Jeremiah also appears on a sherd; but it cannot be said with certainty that it referred to the Prophet. Yet the 'Letters' amplify his account. The potsherd writings are about 500 years older than the Dead Sea Scrolls.

Jeremiah prophesied the fall of Jerusalem, and warned the King of Judah against alliance with Egypt and resistance to Babylon. The pottery letters set out the difficulties of the officer in the out-post, and particularly the trouble caused by a local prophet who spread alarm and despondency. 'His messages are not good, and weaken the hands of the country'. The book of Jeremiah tells of a trouble-maker, one Uriah, who 'prophesied against the city and against the land', and fled to Egypt. He was brought back to Judah under some early procedure of extradition, and was put to death by the King Jehoiakim, who 'slew him with the sword and cast his dead body into the grave of the common people'. Scholars have conjectured that the 'Letters of Lachish', found together in the rubble of a room, which may well have been the guardroom of the fort, were part of the evidence laid before a tribunal that judged there Uriah on the charge of treason. So we are brought back closely by contemporary records to the grim days of the campaign which ended in the destruction of Solomon's Temple and in the First Captivity.

Another flash in the correspondence of the sherds tells how the officer watched in vain for the beacon signals of Azeka, a neighbouring fortress—that must have fallen—and sent his report 'to Lachish'. There in Hebrew letters stands the name of the place for which the archaeologists had patiently searched. The sherds give us a tattered scrap of the picture of the last throes in the struggle between Judah and Babylon. The invader

The New Old Land of Israel

was advancing to the destruction of Jerusalem. The fortresses around were falling; the fall of Lachish was imminent. It came, and the city passed almost out of knowledge until our day.

The 'Letters of Lachish', as the records are called, are written in good biblical Hebrew, and prove surprisingly that Hebrew writing was a common art in those days of the Kingdom of Judah. Half-a-dozen hands wrote on the eighteen sherds in a bold cursive script. Jeremiah tells, indeed, how he wrote a contract for the sale of land in his village during the siege of Jerusalem, and deposited the writing in a jar, just as the Dead Sea Scrolls were placed in jars (Jer. 32.18). Now we have visible and authentic testimony to support his account, and the date of the Letters is certain; a few years before 587 B.C., when Jerusalem was captured and destroyed.

Much older writing was found on the site, in a lower layer of the Tel. It may go back 500 years earlier, that is, to the latter part of the second millennium B.C. These older inscriptions are on a jar and an ewer. They are in the early Phoenician alphabet writing, which is more ancient than the first Hebrew script. The words on the jar tell of the gift to the Canaanite deity, who is mentioned also in the records recovered from the buried temple in the Phoenician sea-port Ugarit in Northern Syria. (See p. 26). Thus they associate the popular religion of Palestine in the days preceding the Kingdom of Judah with the religion of Northern Syria. The inscription has four signs which mark a stage between the Egyptian hieroglyphs, a form of picture writing, and the Phoenician alphabet letters. But the signs have not yet been deciphered. Another writing record of some centuries later, which came to light in the dig, is carved on the face of a step, in a palace of the Age of the Judges, about 1,100 B.C. It shows the first five letters of the Hebrew alphabet in the Phoenician script, and may be just a doodle of a mason, or some scribe or would-be scribe. It is the earliest known example of the Semitic alphabet in the correct order.

A different form of writing was found at Lachish on a bronze dagger in a tomb chamber, which can be dated with some cer-

The Philistine Coast: Lachish and Askalon

tainty as of the end of the Hyksos dynasty of Egypt, 1700—1580 B.C. That is the period of Joseph's going down to Egypt and the oppression of the Children of Israel in Egypt.

Yet another intriguing piece of archaic writing was on a pottery ewer decorated with gazelles. The signs are like those of the Sinai inscriptions, and scholars have interpreted the first word as MTON, meaning gift. The gazelles, it has been noted, are strikingly similar to those on pottery finds at the ancient Troy, by Gallipoli. That suggests again the mingling of the Mycenaean civilization with the Canaanite.

The finds at Lachish have given, moreover, a living picture of the art and social life of the Canaanite and Judean town over a period of a thousand years before the first Captivity. The thousand years cover the eighth and ninth dynasties of the Egyptian Pharaohs, who ruled over Southern Palestine from 1650 to 1300 B.C., the period of Joshua and Judges (1300-1000), and the whole course of the Hebrew Kingdom from 1000 to 600 B.C. Lachish was a small town, on the highway from Egypt to Syria, enclosed within walls of which the circuit is less than a mile. Yet the tombs and the single Temple of the Egyptian period have given works of art and beautiful craft. Besides jewellery of gold and semi-precious stones, which is common in other digs, a unique series of scarabs and seal rings covers the Kings of the two dynasties. One tomb alone gave nearly 200 seals. It is as though an archaeologist in England had lighted on a store of rings of the Sovereigns of England, from Henry VI to the present day. Each scarab has a different design. In one, alligators by the Tree of Life; in another gazelles leaping round a palm; in a third a lion rampant. The craftwork of all is delicate and lovely; and gives the impression of a widespread civilization which 3,000 years ago flourished in the 'fertile crescent'.

Mr. Starkey's expedition had the fortune to uncover also a living picture of the commercial life of Judea in the days of the Kings. Beneath the layer of the Egyptian occupation was a public square, surrounded by a row of shops containing stores of goods which were intact. It was like what was found in

The New Old Land of Israel

Pompeii in Italy, when the lava crust which had overwhelmed the town was removed. In Lachish there were a pottery shop with the tools of the trade, a store of oils and wine with jars bearing the royal stamp: a weaver's store, where the weights of the loom—some of them inscribed with Hebrew letters—lay on the floor, and a large limestone vat for dyeing. The wine store contained a picturesque strainer formed by the head of a gazelle, with holes that must have been used to suck the wine. The jars in the oil-store were marked in Hebrew: 'For the King: from Hebron'—and other towns, and must have contained the royal tithe which was paid in kind. In one of the shops the expedition found a clay seal with an impression as clear as if it had been made a few years ago: 'For Hilkiah, the son of M—'. Hilkiah is the name of the high priest in the reign of King Josiah of Judah, one of the good Kings. It is the name also of the father of the Prophet Jeremiah. Another seal found in the debris was inscribed: 'Gedalia, who is over the house'. It seems certain that it must have belonged to that officer of the King's household who was made Governor of Jerusalem after the destruction of the Temple, and was murdered; and whose murder anniversary is still marked annually by pious Jews as a fast-day.

The seal had been used for the stamping of papyrus sheets, and it seems likely that the Hebrews, as well as the Egyptians, habitually used that flimsy material for their legal documents. Scarcely any, however, of the papyrus records themselves have survived in the Bible land. For Palestine is swept by winter rains; and the humidity played havoc with paper archives; whereas in dry Egypt papyrus had a long life. It was the restriction of war which no doubt cut off supply of the writing material—as it did in England during the World War—, and led to the use of the more durable pottery sherds for military and civil records during the siege. We have indeed a few papyrus scrolls from Palestine dating from the third century B.C., when the country was under the rule of the Egyptian Ptolemies. We may recall that the principal market for papyrus in antiquity

The Philistine Coast: Lachish and Askalon

was the Phoenician town Byblos near the coast of Syria. And Byblos gave its name to the Book of Books, the Bible, because the Greek word for book was taken from the place which supplied the raw material.

The expedition found, too, a cemetery of the same period as the market-place and shops of Lachish. It was the rock-cave containing a pile of 2,000 skulls. Some of them were artificially distorted. Many bore traces of trepanning, and are the earliest example of surgical skill recovered in the Land of Israel, though there are older cases in Jericho. (See p. 131). Experts believe that they are the skulls of the defenders of the fortress, who were massacred when Sennacherib stormed Lachish in the year 701 B.C., as depicted on the monument in the British Museum. Near the burial cave the expedition uncovered a road which was strewn with arrow heads, some of metal and some of bone, bent as they had struck the fortifications. On that same road they found fragments of scale-armour of bronze, such as the Philistines who dwelt in the region must have worn. They found also a bronze crest of a soldier's helmet, which corresponds exactly with the crest depicted on Sennacherib's monument in the Museum.

The ancient history of Lachish comes to an end in the Persian period after the return from the Babylonian Captivity. One of the upper levels of the Tel disclosed the walls of a Persian palace, and a hoard of silver coins stamped with Yahud, the Persian name for Judea. The Persian rulers allowed their Jewish subjects a large measure of autonomy, including the right of minting their own coinage. Within the ruins of the palace also were jars with the seal impression Yahud. They must have contained the tithe of oil and wine which was payable in kind to the ruling power. So this mound over an ancient site, which lacked habitation for two thousand years and more, suddenly gave fresh knowledge of the Bible and of the life and customs of the people who lived in the times of the Bible.

It is characteristic of Israel today that, side by side with the archaeologist's revelation of the social life in the days of the

The New Old Land of Israel

Hebrew patriarchs and the kings of Judah, living settlements and social institutions of the restored nation are established in the same spot. Around the Tel of Lachish, which is right on the border of Israel and Jordan, the Israeli Halutzim, i.e. agricultural pioneers, have planted a group of villages around the centre. Most of them are in the form of a Kibbutz, a collective group of young men and women sharing all things in common. The settlement under the Tel itself is formed by a group who, having finished their national service, keep watch on the frontier while they cultivate the soil. Israel and her neighbours have reversed the position which made Lachish a commanding fortress in the Kingdom of Judah. Then the Jews inhabited the hill country, and Lachish guarded the approach from the plain. Today Israel's villages are in the plains and the foothills, and the strong point of Lachish guards the road coming from the mountains of Hebron that are now in the Kingdom of Jordan.

The urban centre of this new area of settlement, which is called Lachish, is being built, however, on another historic site, Gath of the Philistines, the city of the boasting giant Goliath. That is the place of which it is written in the Bible: 'Tell it not in Gath'. Another Tel, not yet excavated, dominates the township which, since 1955, has sprung up in the plain, and in 1957 had already a population of five thousand. The railway of Beersheba and the pipeline of the Yarkon river, carrying water for irrigation of the Negev, pass through Gath, the black fertile soil is fitted for intensive plantations of cotton, sugar-beet and ground-nuts, factories for ginning and spinning cotton and for sugar are already in operation. Gath is the nodal economic point of some thirty villages, which in a few years may be one hundred. The settlers come mainly from all parts of the Orient and North Africa. On the eastern border, where the region touches the mountains of Hebron in Jordan's territory, they are young soldiers. The industries, the public authorities, the agricultural services, elementary and secondary schools, and a cinema will be at Gath. A town-plan has been approved, with a civic and cultural citadel, a recreation ground, and a swim-

The Philistine Coast: Lachish and Askalon

ming-pool, providentially supplied by a sheltered hollow, and a living quarter for the archaeologists who have begun to explore the Tel. The diggers have already found a sloping glacis of bricks, protecting the city wall; and they ascribe it to the age of Solomon.

In the neighbourhood of Lachish and Gath, on the Philistine coast, the ruins are spread of a port-town which has a continuous history from the Bible time to the present day. Askalon (or Ashkelon) has kept its name and its site through the ages, and has been almost unbrokenly inhabited. Today it is marked for a centre of Israel's development in the Negev. In the Bible it is one of the chief towns of the Philistines, the others being Gaza, Ashdod, Ekron, Gath. Gaza, meaning the strong, was a commanding post and harbour on the frontiers of the desert, and a station on the military road, the Way of the Sea, a thousand years before the Philistines sailed over from Crete or the Greek mainland. It was a fortress in turn of Egyptians and Philistines, Greeks and Romans, Byzantines and Crusaders. It has been occupied since 1948 by the Egyptians—except for four months after Israel's Sinai lightning campaign in October 1956, and her occupation of the 'Gaza strip': from November 1956 to March 1957—and is outside the territory allotted to Israel. The other Philistine sites are all in Israel, and of them Askalon is destined to be again the big town.

A stele of the Pharaoh Ramases II (1291-1280 B.C.)—whom some identify with the Pharaoh of the oppression and the Exodus—in the Temple of Karnak, depicts an Egyptian siege of Askalon, in much the same way as the frieze of Sennacherib depicts the siege of Lachish. Perhaps a hundred years after the siege, the Philistines conquered the city. And though it is recorded by the Judges that the Tribe of Judah captured it and its coast, it was a Philistine city throughout the period of the first Temple. After Alexander the Great subdued the Persian Empire, it attracted Greek settlers who built temples to the Greek Gods and Goddesses. Jewish fishermen of Askalon recently found in the sea a Greek helmet which the scholars ascribe to

The New Old Land of Israel

the fifth or fourth century B.C. That suggests, like the finds of Greek pottery along the coast of Israel, intercourse between the Greek islands and the coast of Palestine before Alexander's conquest of the East. Jonathan the Maccabean prince (c. 120 B.C.) captured the town, but soon again it was an autonomous city-state. King Herod adorned it with splendid buildings in the classical Greek style; it was for him a most favoured town because he was born there.

The Rabbis of the early centuries of the Christian era, which was relatively a tolerant period, removed the ban on Jews living in Askalon. It was not to be regarded as a purely heathen city, and so involving a Jewish resident in impurity. The famous Rabbi Gamaliel and a famous proselyte Onkelos, who translated the Bible into Aramaic, lived there. In the period of the Byzantine Empire and of the early Arab dominion in the Middle East, Askalon was an important commercial and cultural centre, and Jews were still active. The celebrated Jewish traveller from Spain, Benjamin of Tudela, found the community there in the twelfth century. When the Crusaders established the Latin kingdom of Outremer (overseas), in that century, King Baldwin II captured it (1153); and it ranked with Acre and Athlit on the Phoenician coast as a principal port of the Kingdom. Its walls and fortress were razed by the Mameluke conqueror, Baibars, when the Crusaders' power was finally broken. It lost its proud position under the Turks, who gave preference to Gaza.

Lady Hester Stanhope, niece of William Pitt, and the first of a line of adventurous English women, enthralled by the romance of the East, came early in the 19th century to live in Syria and Palestine, and dug in the sands of Askalon for treasure of antiquity. She lighted on a gigantic Roman statue; but her Arab labourers smashed it, hoping to find gold hidden in it. One hundred years later, in the early days of the British Mandate, English archaeologists started more systematically to excavate the site, and found near the surface Greek statues, a sacred pool of the Philistine goddess, and the ruins of Herod's

The Philistine Coast: Lachish and Askalon

Senate-house with its approach of colonnades. But the expedition was interrupted before they had dug to any depth, and most of the antiquities of Askalon are still hidden in the earth.

Today amateur diggers constantly light on records of the past. In 1957 an ancient Synagogue was uncovered on the borders of the 'Gaza Strip', which was then occupied by the Israel Army. As has happened often, the pioneers of a new agricultural settlement, ploughing the soil, laid a furrow of history. The central hall of this synagogue was paved with coloured mosaics, pictures of animals, birds and fruit. In front of the place of the Ark for the Scrolls of the Law there were the Menora, the Shofar (the Ram's horn), and another symbol of the ritual. A box in the corner of the Apse, which must have been the treasury of the synagogue Elders, still contained coins of Justinian I, the Law-codifying Emperor (527-565), and of Tiberius II (580-581), and so established a certain date. Another big synagogue in the area was discovered by Australian soldiers during the first world war. A considerable Jewish community, then, must have survived around Gaza in the Byzantine Empire.

The people of Israel, denied possession of Gaza, have today set about enlarging Askalon, and built modern suburbs around the old ruins. South African Jews have taken the place under their wing, and laid out a garden-city by the sea, Afridar, with tree-lined avenues. In the adjoining industrial zone of Migdal-Gad, they have erected a plant for the water pipes which are the life-line of the Negev. Artesian wells sunk along the coast supply the water, and the pipes conduct it to the new villages. Askalon is marked for a railway junction. The line from Beersheba here joins the main-line that runs up the coast to Haifa, and will carry the mineral wealth of the Negev and the Dead Sea to Israel's principal port. A second harbour, however is to be built a few miles north of Askalon. It is near the site of the Philistine city, Ashdod, where the fish-God, Dagon, had his shrine, and still bears the name. Already a big power-station has been built on the edge of the sea, and is to produce vital electricity for the whole of the Negev. A pier juts out from the station; it has been constructed from millions of cubic meters of rock hurled into the sea. The port of the future will be at the mouth of a large wadi (river-bed), and it will be an outlet for both the agricultural and the mineral production of the Negev, including the potash of the Dead Sea, and, it is hoped, the petrol from Israel's oil-field of Heletz, which is near Askalon.

One part of the prophecy of Zephaniah about Askalon was fulfilled in ancient days. 'Gaza shall be forsaken and Askalon a desolation'. In our day the other part of the prophecy is on the way to fulfilment. 'The coast shall be for a remnant of the sons of Judah. They shall feed thereon. In the houses of Askalon they shall lie down in the evening; for the Lord their God shall turn away their captivity.'

The Central Plain: Dor, Megiddo and Beth Shaan

of ten Hellenistic cities on both sides of the Jordan. They were known as Decapolis (meaning ten cities), and they joined together to maintain their autonomy and the Greek way of life against the Semites, the Phoenicians and Jews, and later, against the Nabatean Arabs. They were supported by Rome, after her conquest, as independent municipalities. The conquering Maccabean King, Alexander Jannaeus, 103-76 B.C., who was resolved to make Judea a maritime power, planted Jews in the town; but forty years later, Pompey, the Roman conqueror of Syria and Palestine, constituted it again a Free City-State. In the first century A.D., probably because of the rise of Caesarea to be the chief town of the Roman Province, Dor lost its importance and much of its population. Its Phoenician-Hebrew name meant habitation; and the decline of the once flourishing town and port made it a by-word. The Roman Pliny, writing his Natural History in the 1st century, calls it an image of ruin. Hieronymus, historian of the 3rd century, noted its desertedness, and Arab geographers from the 9th to 12th century do not mention it.

In the Middle Ages, when Palestine was again a centre of commerce, Dor did not regain its importance as a harbour, because Athlit—or Castellum Peregrinorum, the Castle of the Pilgrims—five miles to the North, was chosen for that service by the Crusaders and the Knights Templar, who arranged the tours of the pilgrims. In recent times it has been settled, first by Arabs and then by Jews. The Arabs renamed it Tantura. It was marked for a Jewish agricultural village and one of the early industrial enterprises of Jewish origin. Baron Edmond de Rothschild, at the end of the nineteenth century, having encouraged the 'colonists' to establish a wine-industry in the land, provided for the building of a factory for glass bottles—for the wine of the Jewish villages—to be made with the sand of the beach. Three thousand years earlier, the Phoenicians on that coast had stumbled on the making of glass from sand. But the modern enterprise failed after a few years, because the area, which adjoined the swamps of the Iskanderun river,

The New Old Land of Israel

(named after Alexander the Great), was infested with Malaria.

Medical science, which has since stamped out this disease in all parts of Israel, had not yet been enlisted in the campaign. Today, however, Tantura, having re-taken the ancient name of Dor, has a healthy Jewish population engaged in both fishing and cultivation of the soil. The Arab inhabitants have gone; and their place is taken by immigrant groups from Rumania and the Oriental communities. In the year of underground activities 1947-8, preceding the Israel War of Independence, the shore was used for gun-running by both Arabs and Jews; and in that guerilla warfare the Jews prevailed.

The fortress of Megiddo, which commands the central section of the Plain, was designed by nature; and the identity of the site has been preserved through the ages. In the period of the British Mandate a scientific expedition of Chicago University set itself to remove the hill layer by layer, and expose its buried treasure. Megiddo is mentioned on a pylon of a famous Egyptian Temple of Thutmoses III, the Egyptian conqueror of Palestine in the 14th century B.C., who defeated there the armies of the Hittites. It is mentioned also in records of the Hittites, and often in the tablets of Tel-el-Amarna (See p. 33) of the next century. Then, 200 years later, it occurs in the record on a triumphal monument of the Pharaoh Shishak (Sheshonk), who fought and conquered Jeroboam, the unworthy son of King Solomon. Megiddo and Taanach belonged to the tribe of Manasseh; but 'the children of Manasseh drove not out the inhabitants of those cities, and the Canaanites did dwell in the land'. (Joshua 17, 12 and Judges 1, 27). Deborah, the Prophetess, roused the children of Israel against Sisera, the Captain of the Host of Hazor, and gathered them in the Central Plain of Jezreel. The army of the Israel tribes fought the Canaanite Kings in Taanach by the waters of Megiddo (Judges 6,10). Six hundred years later, when the power of Egypt was waning, the King of Judah, Josiah the Good, he who caused the Book of the Law to be read to all his people, went out against Pharaoh Necho who was attacking his suzerain the King of Assyria, and fought him

VI

The Central Plain: Dor, Megiddo and Beth Shaan

THE Central Plain of Israel, which runs from the Mediterranean to the Jordan Valley, is called in the Bible the Valley of Jezreel, meaning 'God is the sower'—which is appropriate to its fertility. It is called today simply Emek—the Hebrew for valley. It has been a highway of armies through the ages. The Great North Road from Egypt to Syria, Assyria and Babylon passed up the Philistine coast to the Carmel ridge south of Haifa, there turning at right angles, skirted the ridge by a pass which is called today Wadi Ara, and continued under the Mountains of Ephraim along the Central Plain to the descent to the Jordan. It crossed the river by a bridge at its outlet from the southern end of the Sea of Galilee, and then mounted to the plateau on the east of the rift. The Central Plain was a break in the high plateau between 4,000 and 2,000 feet above sea-level, which started in the snowy mountains of the Lebanon, passed to the less high undulating hills of Galilee, and on the southern side of the Plain became the plateau of Samaria, and further south, the plateau of Judea. It was the battle-ground of antiquity, as Flanders was of modern Europe.

This section of the famous military road of antiquity, the Middle Ages and modern times has been guarded by four fortresses. From west to east they are: Dor by the Mediterranean, Megiddo and Taanach in the middle, and Beth Shaan at the east end. They are natural strong points. Their recorded history goes back to ages before the entry of the Children of

The New Old Land of Israel

Israel into the Promised Land, and they are frequently mentioned on Egyptian and Assyrian monuments. Dor appears, too, in the Egyptian diplomatic archives of Tel Amarna. In the Bible they are named together. Thus in the Book of Kings (1.4), where the Princes of King Solomon are enumerated in an account of the administration of the kingdom, we read that of the twelve District Officers who provided the victuals for the king and his household, each for one month of the year, his son-in-law was responsible for the region of Dor, and another officer was in charge of Taanach. Megiddo and Beth Shaan, have been, while Dor and Taanach have not been, thoroughly excavated in Modern times by the archaeologists. A preliminary digging at Dor, however, by Professor Garstang in the Mandate time, revealed a shrine of the Canaanite-Phoenician goddess, Astarte, and traces of an old Phoenician harbour with the ledges where the galleys were beached. Dor appears to have been the border town between the Phoenician coast to the North and the Philistine coast to the South.

An Egyptian papyrus document of the period of Ramases XI, a Pharaoh of the 12th century B.C., gives a vivid glimpse of Dor—if the place is properly identified. An officer of the Temple of Amon in Egypt, named Wen-Amon, was sent by ship to Syria to fetch cedar wood for the Temple. His boat put in at Dor, where one of the servants stole some gold, and the officer complained to the 'king', or sheikh, and asked him to arrest the thief. The king offered to make a search, and the ship remained nine days in the port. The thief was not found, and the ship had to proceed on its way.

A lovely statue of the Greek goddess Aphrodite was found on the site. It was a work of the classical school of the 5th century B.C., and it may have been brought there by Phoenicians, or possibly by Athenian mariners. We know from a Greek writer of the fourth century that the Athenians had a trading post at Acre, twenty miles to the North.

In the Hellenistic era, when the Middle East was ruled by the successors of Alexander the Great, Dor was one of the League

The Central Plain: Dor, Megiddo and Beth Shaan

at Megiddo, but was slain 608 B.C. (2 Kings 23,29). So much for the written record.

During the last forty years the spade has enlarged that record. First, before the World-War of 1914, a German expedition scratched the surface of the hills of Megiddo and Taanach, and found seals and scarabs of Egypt, Babylon and Assyria. Then an American archaeological enterprise (1925-1932), liberally financed by John Rockefeller, Junior, who founded the Museum in Jerusalem, systematically excavating the vast site, uncovered temple after temple, and most spectacular of all, a vast system of stables for horses. The masonry of the walls that contained the stables was similar to that of the foundation of the walls of the Temple of Solomon in Jerusalem. The Bible says that King Solomon built a store-city in Megiddo, and the scholars were assured that the stables were a part of that city. To make assurance certain, the design which is known as the seal of Solomon was engraved in the walls.

A model of these stables was a showpiece of the Exhibition of the Land of the Bible held in London in 1954. It showed stalls for 300 horses, with mangers and tethering posts of hewn stone. In some of the mangers were grains of corn nearly 3000 years old. The wisdom of Solomon, it seems, embraced horse-breeding as well as the building of a Navy. Megiddo is one of several places where vast stables of his period have been disclosed. When the expedition came to a lower level, they found a treasure trove of intrinsic value, and, what is rare in Palestine digs, of beauty. It was the layer of an Egyptian occupation of the 15th or 14th century B.C., when the site must have been occupied by a palace of the Hyksos princes, or of the governors appointed by them. The treasure contained a heavy gold bowl in the form of a skull, a cosmetic jar of Serpentine, a glass scarab set in a ring of electrum, and a collection of carved ivories depicting animals and human and divine figures, sphinxes and clowns, Maltese crosses and cartwheels. The abundant ivories and the pottery of many designs indicate the gathering in the fortress of the art and culture of Egypt, Meso-

The New Old Land of Israel

potamia and Assyria. One ivory depicts the King going to war in his chariot. Another trophy of Megiddo, from the period of the Kingdom of Judah, was a sculpted capital of a column in what is called the Proto-Ionic style. That means, it corresponded with the early Greek sculpture of Ionia, and suggests that the Greeks borrowed designs for their art as well as their alphabet from Semites.

A remarkable and unexpected find in the site, which had been dug scientifically in recent years, was made in 1955. A broken clay tablet, marked in cuneiform writing, was picked up by a Jewish shepherd of the newly-founded collective village (Kibbutz) at Megiddo, in a heap of debris from the dig of the American Expedition. It proved to be a fragment of a famous Babylonian religious epic. The poem of Gilgamesh, written about 1500 B.C., is one of the earliest literary works of antiquity, much earlier than Homer. Hitherto sections of it, inscribed on tablets, have been unearthed only in Nineveh, the capital of the Assyrian Kings. The finding of the fragment at Megiddo shows that Assyrian culture, as well as Assyrian Armies, had entered Palestine, which was always a meeting-place of civilizations. At Taanach, also, cuneiform tablets were found in the Babylonian language. One of the tablets found on the site affords a remarkable example of mingling cultures. The seal of the author bears a Babylonian name, son of Nergal, the Babylonian god; the legend is in cuneiform writing; and the main text of the tablet is in Egyptian hieroglyphics.

The Hill of Megiddo has been a strong point occupied by all the conquerors of Palestine. It rises above the Wadi Ara Pass, leading from the Coast Plain, where it enters Esdraelon. The Romans held it, and the place took the name Legio, after the presence of their garrison; whence the modern Arab name of the adjoining village, Lejjun. In the Book of Revelations of the New Testament the place where the angels on the Day of Judgment will pour out their vials of wrath has the Hebrew name Armageddon. That is compounded from Har, meaning Hill, and Megiddo. The decisive battle of Allenby's campaign against the

The Central Plain: Dor, Megiddo and Beth Shaan

Turks in 1918, which virtually ended the First World War in the Middle East, was fought at Megiddo, and the victorious English general took his title from the place where the English cavalry surrounded the Turkish Army. Thomas Hardy, bursting into poetry over the victory and its historic Bible scene, wrote:—

"Did they catch as it were in a vision at shut of the day,
When their cavalry smote through the ancient Esdraelon Plain,
And they crossed where the Tishbite stood forth in the enemy's way,
His gaunt mournful Shade as he bade the King haste off amain?"*

The valley of Jezreel (Emek) was an area of intensive Jewish agricultural settlement during the period of the British Mandate for Palestine. Close to the Hill of Megiddo, on another height, the collective village of Mishmar Ha-Emek (meaning the Guard of the Valley) was planted. In the War of Independence, 1948, the Arab Army made a determined attempt to take it; but they were foiled, and could not penetrate the pass and cut the Jewish line on the coastal plain. Today the Mound of Megiddo is on the frontier between Israel and Jordan. The guards perched on the summit of the mound watch every movement. The whole valley, down to the Jordan, is in Israeli hands; but the hills of Ephraim on the east side of the Megiddo pass are in Jordan.

Modern Beth-Shaan, before 1948, was a township half Arab and half Jewish. Now its population is altogether Jewish. The mound of ancient Beth-Shaan is as prominent in the Eastern end of the plain as the hill of Megiddo in the centre. It was known to the Arabs as El Hosn, that is, The Fortress, and it rises like the rock of Gibraltar, high above the plain. Militarily it was the key-place in the Emek, and the Pharaohs kept a garrison in it. In the same way as Megiddo, it was thoroughly explored in the Mandate period by an American expedition.

* The Tishbite is the Prophet Elijah; and the King was Ahab.

The New Old Land of Israel

Egyptian temples and fortresses were disclosed in several strata, which could be dated continuously from 1500 to 1000 B.C. Some of the temples contain monumental tablets recording the exploits of the warrior Pharaohs, Thutmosis (1500 B.C.), Seti I (1350), and Ramases II (1300), who conquered the Canaanites. A feature of these temples was the variety of gods and goddesses whose images were found. Besides the Egyptian, there were the Canaanite Ashtoreth, the Phoenician Mekal, the Philistine Reshef, (who is identified with Dagon the fish-god, and was worshipped along the coast), and the Assyrian Nergal. A basalt panel shows the god Nergal as a lion, and below, the sculptured figure of a dog. Scholars interpreted it to represent the guardian hound keeping off the Assyrian intruder.

The free trade in gods illustrates the history of the empires and the procession of the conquerors and the peoples and their cults. To make a comparison with English history, the Canaanites are in the place of the original Britons; the Egyptians are the Roman conquerors, the Hebrews, who came across the sea of the desert, are the Anglo-Saxons, the Philistines, who came in ships over the Mediterranean, are the Danes, and last, the Assyrians and Babylonians are as the Norman conquerors. Philistine burials in anthropoid clay coffins were found in Beth-Shaan.

The region of Beth-Shaan was the scene of Saul's last battles with the Philistines. He was killed at the battle of Gilboa on the Northern side of the central plain, and his body was brought by the Philistines and hung on the wall of the Temple of Dagon at Beth-Shaan. David avenged the defeat, and Beth-Shaan remained a fortress of the Kingdom of Israel. After the Assyrian captivity of the Children of Israel, c. 700 B.C., however, the Valley of Jezreel was invaded by barbarian hordes from further north, whom the Greeks called the Scythians. That was one of the first big movements of peoples from the Steppes of Eurasia to the Middle East. They were beaten back by the Persians, but their temporary occupation of Beth-Shaan left a name, Scythopolis, which remained throughout the

8. Beth-Shearim, Israel. Archway of the old Sanhedrin hall and Kibbutz of today

Beth-Shearim. Catacomb interior

9. Hazor. A view of the slopes before excavation

Hazor excavation. Citadel mound

10. Caananite shrine, 1800 B.C. found in Hazor excavation

11. Timna. Site of King Solomon's mines

The Basilica of Byzantine Esbeita in the Negev

The Central Plain: Dor, Megiddo and Beth Shaan

Hellenistic and Roman period. Under that name the town, resettled by Greeks, was another member of the Decapolis, like Dor. The archaeologists have revealed a wealth of Greek and Roman ruins, including a vast theatre and a Hippodrome, where early Christians were martyred. They found also pottery like that of Roman Gaul. From the Byzantine period there are the ruins of a circular church, and from a later era the ruins of a Crusader castle.

The East end of the Central Plain was the scene of two decisive battles in world history. The Moslem Arabs, inspired with burning faith, in their first outburst from the peninsula of Arabia in the 7th century, routed the Byzantine Army at the battle of the Yarmuk river, which flows into the Jordan on the East side, opposite the end of the Plain. And the devastating hordes of Mongols, who poured across the Middle East in the fourteenth century, and over-ran the Moslem realms of Iran and Iraq, were defeated at the battle of the Yalud, which is a tributary of the Jordan on the Western side, flowing a few miles below the Mound of Beth-Shaan. The Crusaders erected again a fortress on the Mound, but it was razed by the Saracens. And for 500 years the strong place was abandoned. The country around it went to waste. Jewish settlement in the Upper Jordan Valley at the beginning of the twentieth century brought the beginning of a revival of Baisan, as the Arab village was now called. Then under British rule, the Jewish National Fund for Palestine, an instrument of the Zionists for land purchase, acquired the whole Emek for agricultural settlement. At the same time, lands in the Upper Jordan Valley, which had been owned by the Turkish autocrat Sultan, Abdul Hamid, and on his deposition were declared to be State lands, were transferred by the Government of Palestine to the Arab tenants. Baisan grew in importance as the centre of the district administration, and a market town and a meeting-place of Jews and Arabs.

A railway ran through the Plain from Haifa to the Jordan; and then, passing the Southern end of the Sea of Galilee, mounted to the Eastern Plateau. Baisan was a station on the

The New Old Land of Israel

way to Damascus. The line, laid by the Turks, was a branch of the Hedjaz Pilgrim railway, which was built from Damascus to connect Syria with the Holy Cities of Southern Arabia, the region of the Hedjaz, that is forbidden to Infidels. Nearly a century ago an English enterprise was formed, the Euphrates Valley Railway Company, to build a line from Haifa to Baghdad. And the first part of the track was designed along this central plain. But the project soon fell into trouble and was abandoned. The Ottoman Government took over the enterprise; but laid the line only to Damascus.

The railway service along the Central Plain has been discontinued since the establishment of the State of Israel. The impenetrable barrier of the cold war has rendered it impossible for trains to pass the frontier in the Jordan Valley. So, too, a pipeline, that was laid in the days of the British Mandate from the oilfields in Iraq to the Sea and the Refineries at Haifa, to carry the precious oil, and passed through the Central Plain, has been derelict and unused since 1948. The Government of Iraq cut off the supply. Pylons, however, which carry electricity to all the towns and villages of Israel from a fuel power-house in Haifa, bestride the Plain. The hydro-electric station, which was built during the Mandate on Tel-Or (the Hill of Light), at the end of the Plain, where the Yarmuk river fell in cascades into the Jordan, is also out of action since the establishment of the State of Israel. It stands in the territory of Arab Jordan, and the Jews who worked it may not cross the line. The river Jordan, descending again in twists and turns, in its 200 miles serpentine course to the Dead Sea, was harnessed by the hydro-electric plant. A dam held up the waters of the two rivers in a man-made lake, and thence they were conducted by chutes to create electric power.

New Jewish villages have sprung up in the last years around Beth Shaan. One of them, Beth Alpha, is on the exact site of an old place of Jewish rural habitation dating from the sixth century of the Christian era. That was proved when the settlers began to plough their land, and found the mosaic floor of an

The Central Plain: Dor, Megiddo and Beth Shaan

ancient synagogue with an exact date, 520 A.D. The mosaic, illustrating the signs of the Zodiac, Noah in his Ark, and also Abraham's sacrifice of Isaac, is a vivid example of the folk-art of the Jewish people fifteen hundred years ago, and has a quaint and childlike charm. Surprisingly the figure of the Sun-god, Helios, appears in the middle of the design. The hybrid village name, part Hebrew, part Greek, symbolizes the mixed culture of the age; and so do the inscriptions on the mosaic floor in three languages, Hebrew, Aramaic and Greek.

The Jewish folk-art was mingled with Hellenistic elements, and was to exercise a strong influence on early Byzantine Christian art. In the early centuries of the Christian era, the Jews both in the Land of Israel and Babylon were in the habit of putting in the Synagogues images of living things and human beings. A Rabbinical text of the fourth century says that the depiction of figures in mosaics was not prohibited. The most spectacular Synagogue decoration was found thirty years ago in a buried building of the fifth century at Dura-Europos on the river Euphrates, and comprised magnificent frescoes of Bible scenes.

The popular interest in archaeology among the rural population of Israel is shown again in the establishment of a museum of antiquity at Ain Harod, one of the larger villages of the Central Plain. That village is built by a historic spring where Gideon, the warrior judge, tested his men to see whether they lapped or scooped the water with their hands. The new agricultural settlements of Israel along the plain are living examples of a rebirth of a nation where 3500 years ago it began its history, and for 1500 years made that history part of the heritage of humanity.

VII

Galilee: Hazor and Beth Shearim

✦─────────────────────────────────✦

A BRANCH of the Great North Road of Israel leads from Haifa to Nazareth and the Galilee hills, then, turning eastwards, descends steeply to the Lake of Galilee in the pit of the Jordan Valley, 600 feet below sea-level. From the northern end of the Lake it mounts gradually to the Upper Jordan Valley, which is bordered on either side by a mountain wall. The fertile plain widens into the most northern of the three internal lakes formed by the Jordan, which, until a few years ago, was surrounded by a malarial swamp. That is Lake Huleh, known in the Bible as the Waters of Merom. During the last years the Government of Israel has carried through a scheme of drainage and canalization, which has reclaimed 15,000 acres of marsh, and turned them to fruitful soil. It has left only a small corner of the Lake as a nature reserve. The scheme will be completed by an irrigation canal to take part of the fertilizing waters of the Jordan to the arid Negev. Just before the road reaches the Huleh Lake, a high and vast Tel, bordering a big ditch, rises 200 metres from the plain. From the top you see snow-capped Mount Hermon. And in the summer months you will see some hundreds of workers digging in different sections of the mound, and removing layers of it.

The high road was cut in the period of the Mandate through a shoulder of the mound, in order to get rid of a diversion, and at a period of grave unrest in Syria provide quicker communication with the Syrian frontier. Syria lies some thirty miles

Galilee: Hazor and Beth Shearim

north, beyond Israel's narrow salient that contains the headwaters of the Jordan. The river here cascades through a mysterious black basalt gorge, falling in a few miles 900 feet to the Sea of Galilee. Below the mound is one of the Jewish villages founded by Baron Edmond de Rothschild. It bears the name Ayelet Hashahar, meaning 'deer of the dawn', and it has become the headquarters of the archaeological expedition which is digging the mound. A museum is being established in it of the objects of the dig which are not required by the Israel Government department of Antiquities or the museum of the Hebrew University of Jerusalem.

The mound is the biggest antiquity site in Israel. It covers, or rather, covered—for it is now being uncovered—the fortress city of Hazor, which has a story of four thousand years. Like Megiddo, in the Vale of Jezreel, it was a strong point on the military road between Egypt and the Western Asia Empires, and was also a principal town of the Canaanites. It extends over two hundred acres, whereas Megiddo and Jericho and other famous Tels extend over less than twenty acres. It has been proved that the whole area was once built-up, and inhabited by 40,000 souls. An archaeological expedition, directed by Dr Yigal Yadin, the son of the late Professor Sukenik, the Archaeologist of the Hebrew University and of Dead Sea Scroll fame, is scientifically exploring the whole area. He was himself Chief of Staff of the Army of Israel in the War of Independence, and has abandoned the sword for the spade. He interpreted two of the original Scrolls which his father acquired for the University, and now he directs the largest and the best-equipped expedition in Israel. It started work in the summer of 1955, and was due to continue its field exploration till the winter of the year (1959-60). In the last four years it has disclosed treasures of history, and it has more to give. The treasures were displayed at an exhibition in the British Museum, London, 1958.

Hazor is described in the Book of Joshua (11.11) 'as the head of all the Kingdoms of the (North) Canaanites'. Joshua's victory over King Jabin of Hazor and the destruction of the fortress

The New Old Land of Israel

occurred at the beginning of the 13th century B.C. But the recorded history begins seven hundred years earlier, in Egyptian and Sumerian—(that is, Mesopotamian)—documents. In the archives of Mari, a site on the Euphrates, Hazor appears as a centre of commerce. In Egyptian hieroglyph tablets of about 1800 B.C. it is mentioned as a hostile town to be cursed by magic imprecation. (See Ch. 4). Some hundreds of years later, when Egypt embarked on her imperial expansion northwards, the warrior Pharaohs, Thutmoses III, and Seti I, occupied it in order to guard their line of communications, and proudly mentioned it in their monuments. Then in the 14th century B.C., as Egypt's power weakened, the satellite 'King' of Hazor made himself independent; and the diplomatic documents of Pharaohs, (see p. 33), known as the El Amarna letters, include bitter complaints from the 'King' of Tyre, who was an Egyptian vassal, against him. Egyptian suzerainty had been repudiated before the Children of Israel entered the Promised Land. King Jabin rallied all the kings of the northern league of Canaanites, 'the Amorites, Perizzites, Jebusites and Hivites, and they went out to battle, and all their hosts with them, much people, even as the sand on the seashore in multitude, with horses and chariots very many.

'And when all the kings were met, they came and pitched together at the waters of Merom to fight against Israel. But Joshua fell on them. And the Lord delivered them into the hands of Israel who smote them and chased them to great Sidon (the Phoenician town on the coast). And Joshua at that time turned and took Hazor, and smote the king thereof with the sword . . . And they smote all the souls that were therein, utterly destroying . . . And he burned Hazor with fire.'

Hazor must have been soon rebuilt, because in the Book of Judges we read that another Jabin, King of Hazor, had nine hundred chariots of iron, and he oppressed Israel for twenty years. His captain Sisera was destroyed in the battle against Barak and Deborah, the Prophetess of Israel, on the slopes of Mount Tabor and of Megiddo. 'And the hand of the Children of

Galilee: Hazor and Beth Shearim

Israel prospered and prevailed against Jabin, King of Canaan.' (Judges, 4). This is the story which is being confirmed and amplified by archaeology.

The Tel of Hazor comprises two parts; a citadel with the royal residence and the fortress: and the town in which the people lived. Like the other Tels in the land, it is a book of history to be read backwards. The top layers are the latest in date, and only after they have been examined and removed can the expedition get to the more ancient. The Bible tells that King Solomon rebuilt Hazor (c. 1000 B.C.) as a fortress; and it remained a citadel of the kings of Israel in the northern kingdom, till it was destroyed again by the Assyrian Tiglath Pileser, 732 B.C. Pekah was the wretched king of Israel when it was captured; and the destruction this time of the inhabited city was final. The hilltop of the old citadel, commanding the neighbourhood, was indeed a strong-post again and again through the ages. The Persians who ruled Palestine (550-330 B.C.) left relics of their occupation; so did the Hellenistic and the Roman rulers, and lastly, the English who, at the time of the Arab revolt 1936-9, placed on it a police pill-box.

The site of Hazor had passed, however, from memory till 1928, when the British archaeologist, Professor Garstang, exploring in the footsteps of Joshua from Jericho to the north, had the intuition that this vast mound might be the site of the fortress which Joshua destroyed. His rough soundings in the Tel convinced him that he was right. He thought he had found confirmation, from the pottery that was strewn on the site, for his theory that the Israelite conquest took place in the early part of the 14th century. Then for twenty-seven years nothing more was done to reveal the secrets. Now Dr Yadin, with the generous help of the late James de Rothschild, has been able to initiate a thorough examination.

The published results of the first three years of the dig surpassed expectations of what the site would reveal in the way of religious and social history. It is not sensational, like the treasure of Jericho and the Dead Sea Caves, (see Chs. IX and X)

The New Old Land of Israel

but rather a fitting together, as with a jig-saw puzzle, of hundreds of little pieces. History is reconstructed by big and little things of small intrinsic value; bits of wall and foundations, subterranean chambers and tombs, shrines and sculpted images and tablets, pottery sherds with a name carved or written, animal bones and the skeletons of men, women, and children. Dr Yadin proved in his first year's exploring that Garstang's identification of the site was right, but his dating of the destruction of the Canaanite city was wrong by about a hundred years. Garstang relied on the absence in his superficial soundings of what is known as Mycenaean pottery, i.e. jars and vessels with marks and ornaments of the Greek and Cretan ware. That was spread over the Middle East from the thirteenth century, when the islanders of the Aegean made their way to the Asiatic mainland, and brought their pottery with them. Yadin's exploration unearthed at once numerous pieces of their style in the floors of the city; and the corollary was that the destruction happened during the century when the Europeans had arrived.

The expedition divided its searches between the citadel of twenty-five acres and several selected points in the vast surrounding earthwork which covered the Canaanite city. The citadel comprised, besides the palace, the stone houses of the King's men and the aristocrats. The surrounding urban area was for the 'polloi', the soldiers, workmen, artisans and servants. The middle of the enclosure was the vast parking-place for the chariots and the farming vehicles, and probably the stables. A deep moat, such as is found in the Hittite city of Carchemish in Syria, surrounded it. And it is almost certain that the invading Hittites penetrated to the fortress.

The main dig in the citadel had by 1957 reached the city of King Pekah, dated about 700 B.C., and it may be that a score of cities, marked by bits of wall and chambers of many ages, will be uncovered before the original town, comparable with the original Jericho, is reached at rock bottom. The most startling discoveries hitherto have been from the upper layers, of the

Galilee: Hazor and Beth Shearim

time of the Kings, Solomon, Ahab, Jeroboam II, and Pekah. Rare Hebrew inscriptions, the oldest known in Galilee, were on wine-jars. One was probably part of a tithe, 'for Pekah', with the description of the wine. The Hebrew word occurs in the Song of Songs (2,13), and is there translated 'Tender grape'. Another jar is inscribed, 'for Makhbiram', a Hebrew name hitherto unknown. It was in a house where also a work of domestic art was buried. That was an ornate palette of ivory, with the carving of the Tree of Life on one side, a woman's head on the other, and two stylized birds on each side of the head. Some beautiful specimens of Mycenaean ware, which may have held perfume, and a stopper of a perfume flask, carved in the shape of the Egyptian goddess Hathor, were found also. Dr Yadin conjectures that the house belonged to an important merchant whose wife liked pretty things. The house showed signs of earthquake damage, and the guess is that the earthquake is that mentioned in the first verse of the Israel Prophet Amos, who was contemporary with Jeroboam II. A third inscription was found on a jar, not in the Hebrew but in the older cuneiform script, and may be hundreds of years older. It was just a Semitic name.

The floor of the fortress of Pekah was covered with burned ash, a proof of the utter destruction. In a kitchen the skull of a sow, which must have been caught in the conflagration, and, pathetically, the shell of a tortoise were on the floor. And in a casement of the city wall a big sea-shell, such as are found in the Red Sea, was lying about. It was pierced, so that it might be used as a trumpet to summon the garrison in case of attack. Other household objects were the stone weights of looms—the wooden looms themselves must have been burnt—and a stone gaming-board.

More spectacular objects, illustrating the religious life, were recovered in the enclosure of the Canaanite city beside the citadel. They are not later than the 13th century B.C., when the outer city was destroyed. In the first year the expedition uncovered at the foot of the rampart a Canaanite sanctuary of the moon-god, more complete than any hitherto known. The sculpted figure of the seated god, of which the head had been struck off, but was found nearby, and could be fitted, a number of upright stones—Stelae—one with the figure of a man praying with outstretched arms, a basalt lion figure, similar to that of Hittite monuments, an offering-table and vessels were found close together. During the second year the expedition, digging round the sanctuary, found more rooms and objects connected with the worship, store-chambers with big jars, and a potter's workshop with a potter's wheel of basalt, and with many of the craftsman's works. The religious objects include a clay mask, with holes pierced at the side, so that it could be fastened to a face, and a different cult-emblem, a plaque or standard of bronze, silver-plated, on which was wrought the image of a snake-goddess holding a snake in each hand. Digging down to the rock in another part of the enclosure, they found below the floor of the house many infant burials in jars, with one or two juglets in each jar. In a third section a heavy altar of stone, weighing over five tons, showed above the ground. Removing it, they came to the area of a second Temple, of the sun-god (Baal) which comprised, besides the open court, the paraphernalia of worship, the stone foundation of a High Place, a stand of incense, and an alabaster incense vessel. Again the seated idol of the God, and a disc with a four-rayed star as the emblem. Underground canals were constructed for draining the blood of the sacrifices; and finally, below the foundation of the sacred building, the diggers came to a tunnel hewn out of the rock, which must lead to some chambers.

They found, too, burials of the 16th and 17th century B.C.. which are believed to be of the period of the Hyksos conquerors of Egypt and Palestine, who invaded from the North. The pottery and jewellery buried with the bodies and the scarabs and amulets are of the Middle Bronze Age 1750-1550. Another remarkable find of this period was an inscription in the cuneiform Accadian language of Iraq. It is on a stone representing a cow's liver; and, though it has not yet been deciphered, it is

Galilee: Hazor and Beth Shearim

likely that it represents some magic incantation The priests of the ancient religions used this part of the animal sacrifice to divine a war or to predict good or bad crops.

The third year's digging, however, did not solve that mystery of the underground ways. The tunnel led on, and six branches led out of it; but the diggers had not come to the end, which they believed to be burial chambers of the nobles. The most remarkable find of the year in the citadel sector was the gate of the fortress town in the days of King Solomon. It was built with a gigantic wall twenty metres high, and had six compartments, three on each side, which must have been the guard-rooms. On the outer side was a stone rectangular tower. The structure of the gate was exactly like that discovered years ago at Megiddo, which was also built in the days of King Solomon. That bears out the verse in the Book of Kings (1.9.15): 'This is the reason of the levy which King Solomon raised: to build the House of the Lord, (that is, the Temple), and his own house, and the walls of Jerusalem and Hazor, Megiddo and Gezer.' They discovered, too, below the layers of ashes from the Assyrian destruction, the living quarters of the garrison with a mass of pottery utensils. But the most spectacular find of the year was in the mound of the Canaanite city. Continuing the exploration of the Canaanite temple of the Sun-god, built in the Hittite style, they found a wall of upright basalt tablets; and on the floor was strewn a mass of cult objects, libation tables, pottery and the seated god. The form of the temple in three sections was much the same as the Temple of Solomon in Jerusalem—built 300-400 years later. The outermost porch for the crowd, within it a court for the worshippers, and the innermost court of the Holy of Holies for the priests. In the sanctuary they found four figures of bronze, one male wearing a conical helmet, two female, and one in the form of a bull. We are gathering more and more evidence of the Canaanite religion. They found, too, a scarab seal of the Egyptian Pharaoh Amenophis III, of the 14th century, which suggests the date of this temple.

The New Old Land of Israel

In the fourth year the quest of the mysterious underground passages in the Lower Canaanite City had again to be given up, because the expedition must concentrate on the Citadel mound and on two areas of the Lower City, one where the Temple had been found, and the other where it was hoped to uncover the main gate. The effort was justified. Beneath the area of the orthostat Temple two more shrines were disclosed. The older was built on virgin soil, and is ascribed to the 18th century B.C. The other was 300 years later; and on the floor were pottery figures of the Mycenaean style, and a bull, which was the base of a statue of the God. A second lion orthostat was found in a pit to which it had been thrown apparently by the idol-breakers—the Israelites, or other invaders. The lion is a beautifully sculptured head, a genuine work of art, and strikingly like the stone figures of lions which have been discovered in the Hittite cities of Anatolia. The search for the Gate of the Lower City was rewarded. It was a stone structure of the Middle Bronze Age about the 18th century B.C., and access to it was given by a road built on a strong rampart of basalt boulders.

In the Citadel mound, the most spectacular find of the fourth year was of two Ionic capitals, such as have been discovered on the sites of Israel's royal cities, Megiddo and Samaria. The two columns on which the capitals were carved must have belonged to a palace of the Citadel. In the lower stratum the expedition found another important object of their search, the signs of occupation during the period between the destruction of the Citadel by Joshua and its rebuilding by King Solomon. There was pottery of the early Israel period, of the time of the Judges; and other signs of settlement, but without any fortress wall. There was, too, another High Place, with stands for incense and a jar containing the seated figure of Baal, the War-God, which had been cloven with an axe of another iconoclast.

The broad result of the expedition is to show that Hazor's importance as the capital city of North Canaan lasted between 1800 and 1300 B.C. It was then that the Lower City, covering

Galilee: Hazor and Beth Shearim

180 acres, was occupied. Its downfall came with the total destruction by Joshua, and though King Solomon restored it, he rebuilt only the Acropolis area; and that was finally destroyed by the Assyrian conqueror in the 8th century.

Thanks to the indestructible basalt stone of the region, the Hazor expedition has already given a fuller picture of Canaanite religions and civilization than any of its predecessors. As the science of archaeology progresses, the small objects, which previously escaped attention, are fitted into a pattern. The digging at Hazor is done mainly by recent Jewish immigrants, from Persia, North Africa, and other oriental communities, simple, untutored men and women. They are ideal workers, both because they go slow, and because they have knowledge and love of the Bible, and are elated when they find an object which associates their work with the Bible. The knowledge of the life of the ancient Children of Israel has become almost a substitute of religion in Israel of today. Pride and even passive participation in the discovery of the visible relics of the past give to the Israelis of today a sense of unity with the people of the Bible.

While the Tel of Hazor is revealing a picture of the social life of Galilee in the period before and during the occupation of the Children of Israel, another site in Galilee, which has been scientifically excavated for some years, and is still unexhausted, is giving a vivid picture of the religious and social life of the Jews a thousand years later. Judaism had reached its full development as a universal religion; but the Jewish people, having lost their State and their Temple in Jerusalem, were struggling for survival against Roman tyranny. The knowledge in this instance comes not from a visible Tel above ground, but from hidden tombs; and it started unexpectedly through the fortunate find of an amateur.

Between Haifa and Nazareth the high-road passes through wooded hills, the remains of an ancient forest of oaks. New forests were planted on the treeless hills of the region, in the period of the British Mandate, by the Palestine Government

The New Old Land of Israel

and the Jewish National Fund. One of them was in memory of Lord Balfour, who signed the British Government's Declaration about the Jewish National Home; another bears the name of King George V. Jewish agricultural villages were established amid the old and the new forests. In 1936, when the Arab revolt against the British Administration disturbed the whole country, a Jewish watchman of one of these agricultural settlements, engaged on his patrol, marked an old burial chamber cut in the soft rock. The village at that time bore an Arabic name, Sheikh Abreik, from a local Holy Man whose domed white tomb was on a hillock. But when the burial chamber was explored, it was clear that it had nothing to do with the former Arab inhabitants. Kitchener had noted the caves when he was making a survey of Palestine seventy-five years ago, but did not explore them.

The Chamber, when excavated, led on to others full of stone ossuaries, of which some bore legible inscriptions in Hebrew and in Greek. Professor Mazar, President of the Hebrew University, for four years carried out explorations on the hill and in the rocky slopes which, for miles, fell steeply to a ravine. The operation was interrupted by the world war and Israel's War of Independence. It was resumed in 1953, and has been conducted each year since. Early it became obvious that this was no ordinary burial-place of a small Jewish township of the early centuries of the Christian era, when the cultural centre of the stateless Jewish people was in Galilee. It was a necropolis for Jews of all countries.

The Jewish youth group which settled at Sheikh Abreik in 1936 was remarkable. They were the first graduates of the movement, known as Children and Youth Aliyah, for the rescue of boys and girls in Germany whose life was made intolerable in their native land by the Hitler persecution. They had come to Palestine from middle-class homes of professional and mercantile parents. And they had been brought up in the collective and co-operative villages of the Land of Israel. After two years of education, divided between school and field work,

Galilee: Hazor and Beth Shearim

and of apprenticeship as workers in an existing village, they had to decide on their future. Would they stay on the land, would they form a fresh village of pioneering youth, or would they prefer the urban life of their families? This group, who had been trained in the Kibbutz (collective settlement) of Ain Harod, the place where Gideon, the judge of the Bible story, tested his men, chose to form a new village. It was on rough ground, and nobody knew of its historic significance. By a strange piece of historical association, which is characteristic of Israel, the necropolis of the generations who lived after the destruction of the Judaean state was found in the lands of a village of young men and women of the generation which was recreating the nation and the state.

The young settlers took an active part in the search for the buried historical treasure beneath their land. Further exploration of the subterranean passages opening out from the rocky slopes revealed a vast necropolis, with burials of Jews from all parts of the ancient world during the first centuries of the Christian era. The limits of the city of the dead have not yet been reached. Each year fresh openings are found; and more sarcophagi and more inscriptions, usually rough Graffiti of paint or ink, come to light.

Scholars have long wondered where a famous seat of Jewish learning and of the Supreme Rabbinical Council, the Sanhedrin, in the first centuries of the Christian era after the destruction of the Temple, was situated. It was called in the Talmud Beth Shearim, meaning the House of Gates; and in the history of Josephus appears as Besara, a Greek corruption of the Hebrew. The city was the residence of the most famous of the Rabbinical sages in the latter part of the 2nd century, the Patriarch Judah, 'the Prince'. He was the compiler or editor of the Mishna, the Code of the Oral Law of Judaism. That system of tradition, which supplemented the Books of Scripture, had hitherto not been committed to a written text. The Mishna became in turn the basis of the disputations which are recorded in the two Talmuds, of Jerusalem (which was actually completed at

The New Old Land of Israel

Tiberias in the 4th century), and of Babylon (i.e. the modern Iraq) some centuries later. The seat of the Sanhedrin remained in Galilee, but was moved to Tiberias when Beth Shearim was destroyed in the 4th century by the Romans, following a desperate and unsuccessful Jewish revolt. The Israel scholars are now convinced that they have lighted on the town.

So far the more dramatic discoveries have been, so to say, in the nether world. No manuscripts, no scrolls, no synagogue ornaments have yet been found on the hill, though part of the facade and the foundations and walls of the large basilica-synagogue, with a fine gateway of three arches which may have given the name to the place, have been excavated. And there are walls of other public buildings attached to the Synagogue, which may have been the seat of the Sanhedrin. The rock-cut catacombs seem endless. Each is composed of an open courtyard, from which a stone door, still often swinging on its hinge, leads into a hall or halls and burial chambers. One of them comprises twelve halls with over two hundred graves laid out in three levels. Another has four hundred burial places. Others are just family vaults. Despite warnings inscribed thereon, the tombs and the chambers appear to have been rifled by robbers during the ages; for few objects of value have been found.

Speculation has been rife over a monumental catacomb with a facade of three arches, which was surmounted by an imposing stone stair twenty metres high. In the vault two Hebrew inscriptions are roughly painted: 'Rabbi Simeon', and 'This is the tomb of Rabbi Gamaliel'. These are the names of the two sons of Rabbi Judah; and the inference is that he and his sons were buried in the vault, and the monumental structure was in his honour. A further piece of circumstantial evidence was the finding in the same vault of an inscription: 'Rabbi Anina, the Little'. The Talmud records that the dying patriarch nominated Rabbi Hanina as president of the Sanhedrin. It seems that the inscription marks the place of burial of his successor, the difference in the name being explained by the inability of the

Galilee: Hazor and Beth Shearim

Galilean Jews—as the rabbis tell—to pronounce some of the consonants. They dropped their aitches.

Many of the burials are in stone caskets, or ossuaries, containing the bones of the deceased. It was a regular habit of the Jews, and the Christians, in the early centuries to make place in the tomb-chambers for a fresh burial of a member of the family by collecting the bones of the last, and storing them in a casket. They saved ground in a country which was always tiny.

The decoration of the chambers—with the regular ritual symbols, the candelabra, the Ark for the Scrolls of the Law, the shovel for the incense, the ram's horn, used on solemn occasions, and, less often, the figure of a ship; (the idea of Outward Bound souls was, it seems, thus early accepted), of animals and growing things—has little artistic distinction. It is the popular art of the Jews of Palestine in the early centuries, when they do not appear to have cultivated artistic excellence. One sarcophagus bears the figures of lions of a primitive design. The inscriptions also are for the most part formal epitaphs, with a warning sometimes against rifling the dead, which unhappily was not heeded. More are in Greek than in Hebrew, a few in Aramaic and the Palmyra language. Occasionally Hebrew words are written in Greek characters. The inscriptions show the wide area from which the buried came: Himyar in Southern Arabia, Mesopotamia, Antioch, the Syrian coast. Here was the place in the Holy Land where the pious and the rich of that period liked to be buried, the Mount of Olives in Jerusalem, which was the chosen place in the days of the Commonwealth, being denied.

In 1956 an ornate sarcophagus, decorated with the heads of Greek goddesses, but stamped with the Jewish Menora (candelabra), was found in an underground store. It suggests that the undertaker's firm had a stock which might be sold either to Jew or Gentile. Galilee was the region, as we know, of a mixed multitude. The Hebrew name is short for 'Galil Hagoyim', meaning region of the Gentiles. So, too, in a subterranean store of memorial lamps and glass vessels, many of the lamps bore the sign of the Cross, suggesting that they might be bought by Christian customers, though this burial-ground seems to have been reserved exclusively for Jews. In that period, when the religious tolerance of the pagan Roman Emperors was not yet swept away by the intolerance of an Imperial Christian Church, Jew and Gentile were not separated in their commercial life. Recently and unexpectedly an Arabic inscription was found on the rock. It was a short poem written in black ink by a visitor to the ancient tombs, and he gave the date of his visit as the year 289 of the Moslem era, which corresponds with A.D. 902. It is a simple poem about fate and immortality, and it proves that the site was known as a necropolis in the Middle Ages. Pottery lamps of the same era found in a tomb-chamber suggest that it was occupied by tomb-robbers.

The work of exploration goes on each year; and we shall learn more from it of the social and spiritual conditions of the Jews in the era in which Judaism was being consolidated, so that it was enabled to face the trials of centuries of dispersion, persecution and homelessness.

VIII

The Negev: Beersheba and Elath

BEERSHEBA in the heart of the Negev—the arid southern half of Israel—is one of the oldest cities not only of the Land of Israel, but of antiquity. It is older than Jerusalem or Jaffa. In the Bible we read of it first in the story of the Hebrew Patriarch Abraham, who pitched his tent outside a well that gave the name to the town. For Beersheba means, according to the Bible-story, the Well of the Oath. It was there that Abraham, who, following his vision of the one God, had migrated from Ur of the Chaldees and crossed the River Euphrates into Syria and Canaan, made his pact with Abimelech, King of Gerar (a neighbouring village), about the ownership of the well. One of the Dead Sea scrolls, an Aramaic commentary on the Book of Genesis, gives an embroidered account of their encounters, which were pregnant with the future of the Hebrew tribes and the Promised Land.

In our day archaeologists have proved that organized, permanent, urban settlement by the wells goes much further back, by at least a thousand years. Close to the modern town, on a hill above the river bed, are relics of a large community of the Stone Age. For security the houses were beneath the ground and connected by passage ways. The indications are that this earliest civilization of Beersheba was calcholithic, that is, a mixture of the stone and the copper age. The use of that metal, which man learnt to work for weapons and for cultivation of the soil, was one of the decisive stages of human progress.

The New Old Land of Israel

Smelting furnaces and copper implements and copper maceheads were found amid the houses; the copper may have been brought from mines of Sinai and from the east side of Jordan, and fashioned into tools. And there were works of primitive art fashioned in stone carving. The artistic impulse of man was manifest thus early.

In the days of David and Solomon Beersheba was spoken of as the southernmost place of the kingdom—'From Dan (in the north, by the sources of the Jordan) to Beersheba' was the extent of the cultivated land. We know, however, that the Kingdom of Judah, like the State of Israel today, stretched almost as far again to the south to reach the waters of the Red Sea—in Hebrew the Reed Sea—at the Gulf of Akaba. A thousand years later, the cultivated land and the villages of the Nabatean Arabs, whose main home was in Edom, East of the Dead Sea, stretched far into the arid Negev. Their name means cultivators; and having been originally nomads, like other Arab tribes, they were already masters of agricultural skill. They built dams and terraces of rough stones to contain the winter floods, and sunk wells for subterranean water.

Professor Evenari, one of the botanists of the Hebrew University, working with archaeologists of the University, has in the last years lighted on exciting discoveries of agricultural settlement in an earlier age. Near the ancient road leading to Sinai and the Gulf of Akaba, which has been turned in our day to one of the highways of Israel, they discovered the remains of ancient farms, dating back to the time of the Kingdom of Judah. The date was given by potsherds, which are of the Iron Age, about 900 B.C. The farms had terraced fields, with channels leading from the hillsides to carry the flood water to cisterns. The irrigation system of the Israelites was more primitive than that of the Nabateans. But the discoveries confirm the Bible account of how King Uzziah of Judah made the desert flourish, 'and digged many wells. For he had much cattle and loved husbandry'. (Chron. II, 26.10).

The Nabateans were also a maritime people; and their vessels

The Negev: Beersheba and Elath

sailed the Red Sea. They had, too, an important overland trade with their camels; and their caravans went to Mesopotamia and beyond. Their kingdom, which at one time reached to Damascus in the north and to Gaza in the west, was brought to an end by the Romans in 106 A.D. Their capital city was Petra, 'that rose-red city half as old as time'. It lies in a romantic, almost inaccessible gorge, south-east of the Dead Sea, and its buildings were cut out of the red rock. Strabo, the Roman geographer of the 1st century B.C., described with great admiration their system of government. The citizens settled all their affairs and all their disputes peacefully, and scarcely ever went to law. Their pottery was perhaps the most exquisite and delicate produced by the potter's wheel in antiquity; and it testifies to a high standard of civilization.

In the Roman Empire the highway between Egypt and the Orient, a kind of overland Suez Canal, passed through Beersheba to Gaza and the Mediterranean coast. Shortly before the First World War, T. E. Lawrence (of Arabia) and Sir Leonard Woolley, who is best known for his discovery of Ur of the Chaldees, explored the Negev and the wilderness of Zin, where the Children of Israel wandered after the Exodus. They showed that in the Byzantine Empire the region supported both a rural and urban population. Half-a-dozen towns formed a defence line between the Dead Sea and the Mediterranean, and sustained a large permanent settlement. Most of the inhabitants were Christians, and they built Basilicas, Churches and monasteries. The Romans named the region the Third Palestine. And their legionaries kept off the nomads and assured peace. The imposing ruins of the towns of Abda, Esbeita, and others, with their basilicas, forums, and huge cisterns prove that thousands lived in them in an age when material wants were small, and men were skilful. The thrifty inhabitants brought the land into cultivation by making stone dams and rock reservoirs to store the winter flood.

In 1935 an Anglo-American archaeological team excavated a Tel which was by the site of a busy village—then Auja and

The New Old Land of Israel

now Nissana—on the Israel-Egypt border. In the ruins of two churches they unearthed a mass of papyrus documents, written by soldiers, monks and others between the fourth and seventh centuries. Most were in Greek and Arabic, but a few in Latin. There are letters, wills, legal deeds and military orders, and they throw a vivid light on the social life of this remote Byzantine province. Then as now the military colonists at one and the same time tilled the soil and kept out marauders. From the days of Nehemiah that was the model of frontier villages in the Bible Land.

In the latest years Israel archaeologists, exploring the wild country between Beersheba and the Dead Sea, have found the ruins of two forts of the kingdom of Judah, with walls and towers. The Nabateans also have left traces of their skilful engineering in this desert region, brick dams and brick terraces.

When the Byzantine Empire was overrun by the Arabs of Arabia, burning with the ardour of the new religion of Mohammed, Beersheba—renamed Birosabon—and the country to the south were abandoned again to the nomads. The merchants, pilgrims and peasants were discouraged and vanished. The relics of the development from the Nabatean and the Byzantine age have taught a lesson to the Children of Israel of today who are striving again to make the desert blossom as the rose. The Arab conquest, it is said, swept out Byzantine civilisation as a locust-swarm devastates a cornfield. The epoch of the Crusaders brought a temporary revival. The Frank knights, like the Romans, were concerned to keep open the route between Egypt and Syria, and between the Mediterranean and the Red Sea. They built castles on the high places and restored the cisterns and the cultivation. But when they were finally driven from the Holy Land by the Saracens, the country was again abandoned by the settled inhabitants; and Beersheba became just a green spot in the desert, a watering-place for flocks and herds.

It was not till the latter part of the nineteenth century that the Turkish Government, prompted by officers of the German

The Negev: Beersheba and Elath

military staff, realized the strategic importance of the place which bordered on the frontiers of Egypt. With the help of German engineers they laid out a small modern town with rectangular streets, a shopping centre, a Government building, a Mosque, and a public garden. The new Beersheba was the administrative centre for the nomad Arabs. Then in the First World War, when the Young Turks threw in their lot with the Germans, and threatened to attack the Suez Canal and block the international waterway, they brought the railway to Beersheba by a branch from the Jaffa-Jerusalem line, and carried it another seventy kilometres south of Beersheba, beyond the Egyptian frontier in Sinai. During that war Beersheba was the advance base of the Turks for the invasion of Egypt, and a pivot of the defence of southern Palestine. It was the scene of fierce fighting by Allenby's army in 1917. A British military cemetery recalls the struggle. In the period of the Mandate Allenby's bust stood in the Municipal Garden. The statue, which was the work of a Jewish sculptor, disappeared; but the plinth remains in the garden; and a new statue is being sculpted.

The British Mandatory Government retained the Administrative centre of the southern region in Beersheba, and added a school, a hospital and a municipal office by the side of the Mosque and the Serai of the Turkish period. In the last decade of the Mandate a few Jewish agricultural settlements were planted in the region around the town. These scattered points were to be bastions of the Jewish defence in the War of Independence 1948, against the armies of Egypt, Iraq and Jordan. They held out against immensely superior forces, and they were Israel's best title-deeds to the empty land.

In the division of the Mandated country, which was adopted by the Assembly of the United Nations in 1947, most of the Negev, but not Beersheba itself, was allotted to Israel. When the British Administration left in May 1948, the town was occupied by the Egyptians; but during the period of fierce fighting in the winter of 1948, the Israel army captured it and found an empty shell. The small settled Arab population had fled, and did not return. In 1949 the planning of a bigger Beersheba was begun. The Government of Israel, above all, the Prime Minister David Ben-Gurion, immediately recognized the importance of having a strong settled population rooted in the southern half of the State. The Israel Labour Federation and its construction enterprise, Solel Boneh, set about building a town for a population of twenty thousand inhabitants, which should be expanded till it reached fifty thousand. There was no longer the problem of getting the land, or a problem of getting the people. In the first years of the State the population consisted mainly of the soldier garrison and the camp followers; but soon a vast temporary village of tin huts and tents—Maabara—occupied by immigrants mostly from the Orient and North Africa, spread around the old township. During the last years the place has grown with extraordinary rapidity and according to a plan. The temporary suburb of hutments has disappeared, and been replaced by streets and squares of well-designed solid houses of concrete and stone. The roads of the new quarters are bordered with trees, the houses have gardens bright with flowers, and the water, brought by pipes from the coastal wells, makes the desert blossom as the rose.

Already, by 1958, it was a city of over 40,000 inhabitants, and increasing at the rate of 400 a month. It is entering on a new destiny as one of the chief towns of Israel, another Tel-Aviv. It comprises an industrial zone with large factories for glass, china-clay and chemicals; and among its amenities a hall of culture, a youth hostel, and a museum of local history, placed in the former Mosque. It is, too, a centre of research for the Desert Zone, which is half the territory of Israel. An Institute was opened in 1957 for test purposes, under the joint auspices of the United Nations Educational and Scientific Organization (UNESCO) and the Hebrew University of Jerusalem; and a plant for the use of solar energy by aluminium mirrors was installed.

The railway to Beersheba, which the Turks built in 1914, and which was abandoned during the thirty years of the British

The Negev: Beersheba and Elath

Mandate, has been restored. It was completed in 1956, and a survey was conducted for a line from the southern end of the Dead Sea to the Gulf of Akaba, with a cable-way to link with the Beersheba line. Another enterprise, which was stimulated by Israel's Sinai campaign in 1956 and the Egyptian blockade of the Suez Canal against her ships, and any ships trading with her, is the construction of an oil-pipe-line from Elath to Beersheba. It was completed by April 1957, and oil pumped from a tanker at Elath reached Beersheba amid great rejoicing. A bigger pipe-line to carry oil from the Gulf to the Mediterranean is under construction.

Beersheba is today the centre and the chief city of the whole Negev, which stretches 150 miles to the south. During the last years the plains to the north and south have been brought under intensive cultivation by collective and co-operative groups of settlers. Water for irrigation is carried by pipe-lines from springs and wells of the coastal plain, and since 1955, from the perennial river Yarkon that flows to the north of Tel-Aviv. The cisterns and reservoirs from past ages have been reinstated and enlarged. The ring of agricultural settlements has converted a desolate region into the likeness of the corn-belt of the Middle West of America. Archaeologists have proved that in the early centuries of the Christian era the Nabatean Arabs established hundreds of villages in the Negev, and many of these points are used or marked for Jewish settlement. At the same time, tribes of the Bedu Arabs within Israel territory, numbering fifteen thousand, retain their cultivation and grazing areas, and are more prosperous than they have ever been. The Israel Government helps them to cultivate scientifically, and to build stone houses, and provides health services, schools and teachers.

Mr. Ben-Gurion, the Prime Minister of Israel, in 1953 retired, after five and a half years at the helm of the State, to a small rough settlement of sheep-farmers at Sdeh Boker (Cowboy's meadow), thirty miles south of Beersheba, to be a shepherd and get spiritual refreshment. He gave a personal example of his

The New Old Land of Israel

faith in the destiny of Israeli youth to conquer the desert. After fifteen months he was called back to political office, but his example moved many young men and women. And he remains a member of the collective village.

The road from Beersheba to his Kibbutz passes by a vast concrete reservoir, which is filled by the flood waters from the hills in the winter, and is used for irrigation. The site, Tel Yeruham, is traditionally the place where Hagar, the hand-maid of Abraham, came with her child Ishmael, when she was wandering in the wilderness of Beersheba. She had despaired of finding water for the child and placed him under a shrub to die; but the Angel of God called to her, and she saw a well of water, and gave the lad drink. The prophet Elijah, too, fleeing from the wrath of the idolatrous queen Jezebel of Israel, found refuge in this wilderness.

Today Tel Yeruham is a place of settled habitation, at the crossing of three main-roads in the Negev. One goes east to the southern end of the Dead Sea, another south-west to the phosphate fields. A third, the longest, runs 150 miles south-east, the whole length of the triangle of the Negev, which tapers to a narrow point, to Elath at the head of the Gulf of Akaba. In January 1958 the metalled and asphalted road was opened as a new highway for enterprise. It mounts from Cowboy's Meadow to the top of the pass, the Peak of Ramon, 1,000 metres high, the second highest point in Israel, which commands the desert and three 'craters', deep hollows in the shape of gigantic ovals, surrounded by hills. The craters are the result of ages of erosion. It is the land described in the Bible: 'whose stones are iron, and out of whose hills you dig copper'. Mineral wealth has been stored in these bowls from primeval days, as the rainbow colours of the mountain walls indicate: the black flint, the green copper belt, red streaks of iron, gleaming white patches of mica sand, and here and there grey and pink granite.

The mineral wealth of the Negev, particularly copper and iron which were exploited by King Solomon, is being worked again. New forms of minerals, unknown in Bible times, like

The Negev: Beersheba and Elath

flint, clay and mica sand, which are good for the manufacture of pottery and glass, and phosphates, which are a fertilizer, are harnessed to manufacturing use. They are transported to Beersheba along roads which often follow the lines of the Roman highways, and thence to factories around Haifa.

The most spectacular road leads from Beersheba to the southern area of the Dead Sea and to the plant for extracting the minerals in solution from the Sea. Opened in 1953, it descends from the plateau 1500 feet above sea-level, to the abyss nearly 1500 feet below it. The scenery passes from rolling hills and waterless valleys, covered by broom and rough grass, to the desert gorge and canyon of the Arraba, which is a continuation of the Dead Sea, and has a fantastic look like the mountains of the Moon. A steady stream of lorries passes along it carrying potash. For the traditional site of Sodom and Gomorrah at the southern end of the Sea has become a busy industrial area. Before the War of Independence 1948, the main plant of the Potash Company was at the northern shore of the Dead Sea, which is Jordan territory; but that was wrecked by the Arabs in the struggle; and the plant at the southern end, which is in Israel, has been enlarged. The heavily laden waters of what is called in Hebrew the Sea of Salt are carried by canals to open pans, and the potash, bromide and magnesium which they contain are separated from the common salt. Some hundreds of workers are employed in that torrid abyss; permanent housing for them is being built in the new township of Dimona, on the less torrid plateau half way to Beersheba.

Close to the southern shore of the Sea, amidst the utter desolation, an oasis of date palms and tamarisk bushes suddenly springs to the eye. It is the Zoar of the Bible, the city to which Abraham's brother Lot and his family fled when Sodom was destroyed. In the Talmudic era and the Middle Ages it had a Jewish settlement and synagogues, so remote from the world that the Christian persecutors could not reach them. An Arab geographer of Jerusalem, who wrote in the 10th century, described Zoar in that time. 'It is a hot city lying in the hot country, situated near the desert, but it is full of good things. They grow there indigo. The trade of the place is considerable, and its markets are much frequented.' A medieval Hebrew inscription from Zoar is now in the Rockefeller Museum of Jerusalem. In those days Zoar was a stage in the trade route from Palestine to the Red Sea; and Jews were among the merchants. Today its inhabitants include no Jews. For it is situated within the border of Jordan, across the notional line through the centre of the rift that separates the two States. The rift continuing to the south mounts slowly 1500 feet, to fall gradually to the sea-level at the Gulf of Akaba.

The Gulf, leading to the Red Sea, was the principal outlet of the kingdom of Judah to the ocean. The strong kings of Judah firmly held the Negev desert. So we read that Uzziah built towns in the Wilderness and hewed out many cisterns (2 Chr. 26). The Philistines in the southern, and the Phoenicians in the northern, section of the Mediterranean coast commanded the harbours on the western sea. Though Jaffa, after David's and Solomon's victories over the Philistines, was included in the kingdom, the commerce of Judah with Asia and the east coast of Africa was carried to and from another port. 'Solomon made a navy of ships in Etzion Geber, which is beside Elath, on the shore of the Red Sea in the Land of Edom . . . And they came to Ophir, and fetched gold from there' (1 Kings 9.26). He worked the copper and iron of the Negev and exchanged them for gold from Africa. Professor Gluck, formerly of the United States Oriental School, who traced the Bible sites on the east side of Jordan and in the Negev, found not only the remains of a township of King Solomon's time, but also black slag-heaps, relics of a foundry where the slaves smelted the metal. Here was Etzion Geber, meaning the Giant's Spine, and named from great rocks which strew the plain. The site was chosen where the wind blowing from the Dead Sea was strongest, and the flues were constructed above the hearth on the principle of the blast furnace. Intense heat must have been generated, and the slaves who worked the furnace suffered the pains of hell.

The Negev: Beersheba and Elath

Jehosophat and Uzziah, kings of Judah, likewise maintained their fleet in the Gulf of Akaba. Jehosophat sent ships of Tarshish to Ophir for gold, but they were broken at Etzion (1 Kings 22.48). In a later age the Romans made Elath, which they renamed Aila, a strong point of their frontier against the nomad Arab tribes and a port for their galleys sailing down the Red Sea. The Tenth Legion was moved there from Jerusalem at the end of the third century. The site of Aila or Elath was constantly shifting, sometimes to the western, sometimes to the eastern shore. The name also was changed more than once; and Akaba, which till 1949 was the only town at the head of the Gulf, and is on the eastern shore in Jordan, was a shortened form of Akabat—meaning the descent to—Elath. From the Middle Ages till recent years the town was an important station on the Moslem Pilgrim Way for those coming from western Asia and Egypt, and was protected by a castle. The Way ran along the East coast of the Gulf to the Hedjaz, now part of Saudi Arabia, and to the Holy Cities of Mecca and Medina.

Today history has repeated itself. Israel is establishing, on the West side of the Gulf of Akaba, her port and window to the east, close to the site of Solomon's port town, though her principal harbour is at Haifa on the Mediterranean coast. There the ships, bringing the immigrants and imports of all kinds and the reparation goods from Germany, discharge their passengers and their cargo, and load Israel's oranges and industrial exports. But Israel is fast building on the other shore a port that will one day be an important outlet to the countries of Asia and Africa, her link with Aden and Ethiopia, with India and the Far East. Her ships will carry from there the minerals extracted from the Dead Sea and the mines of the Negev. It will be to her what Marseilles is to France.

The new port has resumed the Bible name of Elath, meaning terebinth trees, and is a most romantic spot. The desert scene, with its ring of mountains, is stupendous, and the human energy displayed during the last years in the building

The New Old Land of Israel

of a town and harbour matches it. The place has, too, its strategic importance. In a space of twenty miles around the horseshoe crescent of the Gulf four States meet. Each has a toe-hold; on the east-side Saudi Arabia and Jordan, on the West Egypt and Israel. In March 1949, when a detachment of the Israel Army swept to the southern tip of Negev and occupied the coast-strip of ten kilometres, which had been part of the Palestine Mandated territory, there was nothing but sand and a police post. Today Elath is a growing town, with a municipality, three thousand settled civilian inhabitants and increasing every month, an airfield and a barracks, an embryo port, a botanical garden, where the trees and plants of the desert grow, a marine museum, where an amazing variety of fishes and shells of rainbow hues are displayed, an amphitheatre for concerts, dramatic performances and festivals. And the big artists come. Its buildings and its population give a feeling of the wild west—of the films. Young men and women walk in the streets with pistols in their belts. But today it has good communications with the rest of Israel, both by air and by the motor-road to Tel-Aviv and Jerusalem. A handsome modern building is a cultural centre and club, bearing the name of the American Labour leader, Philip Murray, and being the gift of American Jews to the town. Bare volcanic peaks, red, green, gold and black, tower around. The turquoise-blue waters of the land-locked gulf are stocked with every species of fish, and lined with every form of coral. The Israelis are concerned to develop the fishing, and groups of fishermen, Jewish and Gentile, are settled by the shore.

Cultivation all the year round is possible near the rift valley where subterranean water can be tapped. Young Israelis have planted settlements in spots which appear on ancient maps to have been stations on the Roman-Byzantine highway. At one place, now known as Bir-Ora (the Well of Light), twenty miles north of Elath, a perennial spring has produced an oasis. Groups of youth, doing their pre-military training, reclaim the salt-impregnated waste. With fresh water they literally wash the

The Negev: Beersheba and Elath

salt out of the soil, yard by yard, and then grow fresh fruit and vegetables for the town.

Since the Sinai Campaign 1956, the Israelis have created by the shore of Elath oil tanks for storing petrol on a large scale, the oil being pumped from tankers in the roadstead. They have completed the laying of a pipe to carry the oil to Beersheba and beyond. A few miles south of the tank area, and almost on the Egyptian frontier, a cliff of solid grey, green, and pink granite is being worked, the beginning of a new export industry. The granite blocks are sawn by a fascinating machine, a wedge of seven knives which cut slowly and relentlessly. A bearded Yemenite Jew polishes the slabs with a hand-worked lathe, and prepares them for the American market. In the northern direction from Elath another scene of industry breaks the desert landscape. In the foothills of the Arraba you suddenly see the chimneys and towers and the tanks of a modern smelting plant. That is Timnah, and is close to King Solomon's copper mines. The copper ore is brought here for processing into pure copper. The machinery comes largely from Germany, being part of the reparations which the German Federal Republic is delivering to Israel as material indemnity for the terrible things done to the Jews by the Nazis. The hillside is carved by nature into pillars of red sandstone which guard the entrance into deep caves. Solomon's name is given to the pillars as to everything wonderful in this region.

South of Elath, on the western shore of the Gulf, the Egyptian post of Dahab was occupied by Israel Forces in November 1956. The Israeli archaeologists followed and explored the site. They found a large Nabatean cemetery of the first century and traces of a big settlement. Dahab is possibly the site of the wanderings of the Children of Israel, Dizahab, mentioned in the first verse of the Book of Deuteronomy.

They surveyed, too, an island at the southern end of the Gulf, which is today called Tiran, but in the early centuries of the Christian era had the Hebrew name of Jotba. Here, after the destruction of the Jewish State, a small group of Jews took

The New Old Land of Israel

refuge, and made themselves an independent self-governing community beyond the reach of the Roman oppressor, till the Emperor Justinian, their remorseless enemy, in the 5th century, destroyed the fortress and its defenders.

12. Beersheba. The Turkish Mosque and municipal garden

Gulf of Akaba, Israel

13. *Left:* One of the Biblical scrolls discovered in a cave near the Dead Sea

Below: Pottery jars in which the scrolls were found

14. Jericho. The main trench on the west side of the mound looking towards the Mount of Temptation

15. Potash works at Sodom by the Dead Sea

Massada on the Dead Sea, last Jewish stronghold against the Romans

IX

Jericho and Beth Yerah

JERICHO is the oldest and the lowliest city in the world. It lies a few miles north from the Dead Sea, the lowest place on the earth's surface, 1300 feet below sea-level. It is only in the latest years that the secret of its great age has been fully revealed. The Tel of Biblical Jericho, formed by the ruins and debris of generations, had been excavated, for over forty years before the second world war, with great thoroughness by English and German expeditions. It had been demonstrated that Jericho was a place of ancient worship of the Moon—in Hebrew, Jerah, whence its name—and that the site had been occupied for centuries by Canaanite tribes who were under the sovereignty of the Egyptian Pharaohs, from early in the second millennium till the time of the Israelite invasion. The excavations confirmed the record of Egyptian monuments and the Bible. Fragments of a wall, dated by the archaeologists as of the fourteenth or thirteenth century B.C., which is the generally accepted period of Israel's conquest of Canaan, showed abundant signs of burning. And after that period there was a long gap in the record of occupation, confirming that the curse put on the site of the destroyed city of Joshua was effective. The Bible story of the siege, the falling of the walls, and the destruction of the Canaanite town by the Children of Israel after crossing Jordan to conquer the Promised Land, seemed to be strikingly verified, though the fuller searching of today has thrown doubt on the identification and dating of these fragments of tumbled walls.

The New Old Land of Israel

Yet, it was only recently, after Dr Kathleen Kenyon, archaeologist daughter of a famous director of the British Museum, had carried out successive seasons of excavation from 1952, for the Palestine Exploration Fund, that the unexpected and unexampled evidence of a walled city, going back to 8000 B.C., and of the varied civilization of the mesolithic (middle Stone) and the neolithic (the later Stone) Age, was disclosed. It can be asserted with assurance, in our present state of knowledge of antiquity, that this sheltered spot by a perennial spring—later named after the Prophet Elisha—and a fertile oasis in the rift between the Mountains of Moab and Gilead to the east, and the Mountains and Wilderness of Judea on the west, was the first town in which man regularly cultivated the soil, established a permanent habitation, and built towers and walls for defence. The Tel is a history book of nearly 10,000 years, read in reverse.

Before the discovery of the City of Jericho the oldest villages known were in the region of Ur of the Chaldees, part of what is called the Fertile Crescent. The valley between two great rivers, the Euphrates and the Tigris, was the scene of a town civilization 5000—4000 B.C. Now we have proof that thousands of years earlier, in the much less fertile valley of the Jordan, a primitive race of hunters and cultivators built themselves a walled permanent shelter against the attack of wild animals or hostile tribes. Their city was situated by the copious fountain, which is still copious, and occupied some eight acres. It was four hundred yards in length, and two hundred in breadth, and, it is calculated, would shelter three thousand souls. Though they had only implements of stone, they were skilful builders. It was thousands of years before man discovered how to use metals for his service. Yet they built a town wall, still standing, twenty feet high. At the corner of the wall was a circular stone-built tower, forty feet in diameter, as massive as the bastion of a medieval castle, and within it a stone-cut staircase. In front of the wall they dug a ditch, thirty feet broad and eight feet deep, in the solid rock. The stone staircase of the tower de-

Jericho and Beth Yerah

scended into the heart of the fortress, and at the bottom opened into a passage leading to the town within the wall. It is conjectured that the passage led to the vital water-supply. Similar subterranean passages, but thousands of years later in date, have been found below the city of Jerusalem and the Canaanite city of Gezer in the Judean foothills. (See Chs. II and IV).

The walls of Jericho are two thousand years older than the oldest Pyramids in Egypt. They enormously extend in time our picture of human achievement. These first citizens inhabited no mean city. They had houses with regular straight walls made of mud bricks; and of an earlier age, with round walls; and plaster floors with a burnished surface. The rooms were built round the courtyard and included storage chambers. The doorways show sockets, which must have had wooden posts, and the floor was covered with rush mats, which survive only as a pattern in the earth, but clear enough to show the weaving of the rushes and the cross-stitches which held them together.

Not many miles away in the Jordan Valley the archaeologists have dug up in recent years the traces of a primitive culture which must go back to the same period, 8000—6000 B.C. It was an open settlement of mesolithic men who practised agriculture with flint instruments. The civilization is called Natufian, after the name of a valley in Palestine. And below the wall and town of primeval Jericho, Miss Kenyon has found similar flint weapons and tools, and a harpoon for fishing.

Already in that remote age man had the aspiration and the capacity for expression in some form of art. The burial chambers of the most ancient layers of the Jericho Tel contain a number of plastered skulls, which were unmistakeably designed to be portraits of the dead, and to preserve their features for the family or clan. Part of the plaster was still flesh-coloured, and cowry shells were used for the eyes. One skull bore a painted moustache, though most were clean-shaven. Several of the skulls were trepanned, the oldest examples of a surgical operation. One is of a woman, the Venus of Jericho. The moulders of the skulls were the first portrait artists in history. The primitive inhabitants of New Guinea in our day preserve in the same way the likeness of their ancestors. There were, too, in the oldest levels, signs of an ancient sanctuary: sockets for poles, probably totem poles, though none of these remained.

Above the oldest town-wall of Jericho are relics of a later but less advanced civilization. Man had in this later age lighted on the revolutionary invention of the potter's wheel, and could make all kinds of vessels. But the art of building had declined. The walls of the second Jericho were less strong, and the bricks of the houses were inferior. Miss Kenyon had noted that 'the lower—and older—we go, the more solid the houses'. In the next period of civilization man advanced another big step. He discovered copper and the art of smelting, and could make implements of bronze. And he was continually fighting. The mound of Jericho has disclosed no less than seventeen town-walls, built during the thousand years period of the Early Bronze Age, 3000—2000 B.C., on the ruins of each other. Perhaps earthquake, perhaps invaders from other towns, perhaps nomads were the destroyers.

The next stage of the occupation of Jericho was by a nomad race, which has been identified with the Amorites of the Bible. They came from Syria, and invaded the country with other nomadic peoples who are classed together as Canaanites. They were destructive like the hordes of the Scythians, the Huns and the Tartars, who many centuries later burst on the cradle of civilization and wrought havoc. Egypt, which had meantime become a Great Power, was beginning to extend her rule over a land that was the highway to the north. For two thousand years the struggle was waged between the imperial people of the Nile Valley and the warring peoples of the Valley of the Euphrates and Western Asia, the Sumerians, the Hittites, the Assyrians, and the Babylonians. And so we have come to the age of which the events are recorded in the Hebrew Bible. The mound of Jericho was by this time seventy feet high, the debris having piled up. A street had to be fashioned from the spring

Jericho and Beth Yerah

to the city on the hill. It was made of cobbled steps, such as have remained till our day the pattern in the walled towns of the Bible land, notably in the Old City of Jerusalem.

It was the age of the Hebrew patriarchs, Abraham, Isaac and Jacob; and Abraham's brother, Lot, lived in the Jordan Valley. Miss Kenyon has enriched again our knowledge of the age, its way of life, its arts and crafts, beyond all expectation. The valley in that age must have been dotted with villages. She discovered a honeycomb of tombs in the limestone hills around the Tel, and the chambers of the dead give knowledge of the living. The chambers were revealed by another fortunate accident. Some Arab refugees, who had fled from the territory of Israel during the war of 1948, and were living in wretched encampments, wished, like their ancestors of 8000 B.C., to make for themselves a more human habitation. Hewing for this purpose the soft limestone in hills near the camp, they struck into a hollow place, and to their amazement saw skeletons laid out in a cave or cutting of the rock. Word of the find came quickly to Miss Kenyon, and she started a systematic exploration. Digging on either side of the first cutting, she came across many burial chambers with skeletons and skulls. By the pottery found in them they could be dated as of the early centuries of the second millennium. The furniture, the vases, and utensils, even food and drink in the chambers, were miraculously preserved. The extraordinary volcanic formation of the Jordan Valley, and the presence in the atmosphere of five times the normal quantity of carbon dioxide, had the effect of an antibiotic like penicillin. Not only the wooden biers, the wooden furniture, the alabaster vessels, the linen wrappings, and the woven mats, but even the meat offerings and the drink offerings, which were placed with the skeletons for their refreshment in the after-life, were almost intact. The women of those ages were already concerned with the adornment of their hair and face, and amongst the furniture was a table covered with metal and wooden combs and the fragment of a wig.

In other chambers, where the skeletons were laid out neatly,

The New Old Land of Israel

a bronze dagger lay on the ground, and sometimes a bronze fillet, which may have been an emblem of honour. By the woman's skull, bronze pins and beads. Occasionally more precious and beautiful ornaments, a gold ring set with amethysts, and wooden boxes inlaid with bone carving. A water-pot was in every tomb, often equipped with a dipper jug. In some the reed mat, which covered the skeleton, had disappeared; but the Sherlock Holmes skill of the archaeologist, master of what is called 'environmental archaeology', traced the march of the termite ants which had made their way into the chamber and devoured the vegetable matter.

The craftsmanship of the objects in the chambers was such as has been found in Egyptian tombs, less splendid, of course, than that of the Kings of Egypt, which culminated in the wonders of the tomb of Tutankhamen. But there was evidence from scarabs and signet rings that the Egyptian Pharaohs had their officers in Jericho. In the centuries in which the patriarchs migrated to Canaan, and from Canaan to Egypt, they were rulers in the Jordan Valley as well as in the coastal plain of Palestine. The Semitic dynasty of the Hyksos, who came from Western Asia and conquered Egypt about 1700, made Jericho a strong fortress. They built a slippery plastered glacis at the side of the mound, and on the top of it a crowning wall. A sign of their presence in Jericho is that some burial chambers contained the heads of horses. That feature is found in Egyptian graves in the Tels around Gaza which cover the ancient Hyksos fortresses. The conquest of the Middle East was won by the use of horse chariots; and they loved their horses as today the Arab Sheikhs love them.

The traces of ruined walls in the mound of Jericho show a continuous occupation of the site till 1400 B.C. Then, following the destruction by Joshua and the Children of Israel, there is a long gap. One tomb was found with pottery of the tenth century, the period of David and Solomon. And the Bible tells that in the reign of Ahab, the idolatrous king of Israel, the city was rebuilt. Zedekiah, the last King of Judah, fled to the plains of

Jericho and Beth Yerah

Jericho. And the book of Ezra records that among those who returned from the Babylonian Captivity were 350 men of Jericho (Ezra. 2.34). Yet it was not till the Hellenistic age, a thousand years from the time of Joshua, that Jericho became again an important place of habitation. Its seductive winter climate and its generous vegetation then made it a favoured spot. The later Maccabean princes and the Idumean Herod, who supplanted them, followed the Greek way of life; and Herod built there a winter palace, which he named Cypros. The Roman overlords, too, preferred it to the bleak and turbulent Jerusalem. Josephus, the Jewish historian of the first century, tells us that Cleopatra, Queen of Egypt, coveted its gardens, and received it as a present from her enthralled Mark Antony. But when the Egyptian Queen was removed from the scene, Herod marked the place for his own. The palms and the balsam trees, from which comes the balm of Gilead, the fruit orchards and the gardens of Jericho, were famous through the Roman world. Josephus described the place as a paradise on earth.

Strabo, too, the Roman geographer already mentioned, wrote eloquently about Jericho. 'It is a place surrounded by a ring of mountains. Here are palm groves, mixed with all kind of fruitful and cultivated trees, everywhere watered by streams, and full of dwellings. There are also palaces and a park of balsam. They make incisions in the bark of the Balsam trees, and catch the juice which is remarkable for the cure of headaches and dimness of sight. It is precious also for the resin that is produced nowhere else.'

Jesus passed through Jericho on his way from Galilee to Jerusalem: and the Mount of Temptation, where traditionally he was tempted by the devil, rises steeply above the valley. Queen Helena, the Christian mother of the Roman Emperor Constantine (c. 300 A.D.), and a British princess, built a monastery on that hill. It stands to this day.

Of Herod's palace, theatre and hippodrome nothing remains, and the mound by the spring was not to be a centre of defence

The New Old Land of Israel

or of habitation again till modern times. It was desolate; but the oasis produced by the waters of the spring continued to attract Jew and Gentile. A few miles north-east of the Tel, where another spring, Ain Duk, bursts out, the site of a Jewish community of the early centuries was revealed by an exploding shell during the First World War, when Allenby's army advanced up the Jordan Valley. The shell exposed the mosaic floor of a large synagogue with the Jewish emblem of the Menora (the seven-branched candelabra), and with Hebrew inscriptions. Then, in the latter years of the British Mandate, an Arab farmer of Jericho, who was ploughing land near the Tel for a banana plantation, struck the ruins of another synagogue, which could be dated to the early centuries of the Christian era.

After the Moslem conquest of Palestine by the Arab Caliphs, whose capital in the seventh century was at Damascus, the region of Jericho again enjoyed royal favour. British and Arab archaeologists, digging a mound some miles north of the Tel, some twenty years ago uncovered a palace with exquisite Arabesque carving on its walls, and equipped with baths and pleasure pavilions. It is amongst the most beautiful buildings of which relics have survived in the Holy Land; and it is comparable with another palace, Meshatta across Jordan, which was discovered before the First World War by a German expedition. The palace of Mefjir was a winter resort of the Omayad Caliphs, who, it seems, liked to escape from their crowded capital of Damascus to the free spaces of the Jordan Valley. Their patronage of craftsmen of the subject peoples, Byzantine, Syrian and Persian, encouraged a flowering of the arts in the eighth century, as many sites in Syria and Palestine testify. East and West happily met. The date of this palace and the name of the ruler for whom it was built are certain because they are inscribed on the walls. He was the son of Caliph Abdul Malik, who built in that century the lovely Dome of the Rock in Jerusalem on the site of the Jewish Temple.

The palace was not completed when an earthquake laid it in

Jericho and Beth Yerah

ruins, and the site was abandoned. The remarkable features of the ruined building are beautiful plasterwork, the use of human and animal figures as part of the architectural decoration, and coloured mosaic floors in perfect preservation. One shows a lemon tree with gazelles and lions, another had a design like a Persian carpet. Many Greek inscriptions have been found amid the ruins; others are in Hebrew and Arabic. Portions of Christian churches which bear the Byzantine cross, and must have been multiplied in the neighbourhood, were used by the builders. Within the grounds of the palace baths were fed by an aqueduct which brought the water from the Mount of Temptation above Jericho. The grounds also contained a Mosque having the octagon shape of the Dome of the Rock in Jerusalem.

The Omayad dynasty reached its zenith at this time and soon declined. A few years after an earthquake ruined the palace, the sceptre of Islam passed to other Caliphs who made their capital in Baghdad. And Jericho became just a village till our era of archaeology restored its fame. Today it is bigger than it has been probably since the time of Herod and Cleopatra. North and South of the old Tel a new township has sprung up since 1948, occupied by the Arab refugees from Western Palestine. They were originally living in tents and huts, and were maintained by the United Nations Relief Agency. As the years passed, some of them, as we have seen, built for themselves houses from the limestone in which, four thousand years before, the residents of Jericho had cut their tomb-chambers. The modern village of Jericho—Eriha for the Arabs—is a winter resort, and has again, as in the days of Herod and the Romans, flowery gardens and avenues of palms. By the spring of Elisha itself, under the Tel, the archaeological team of Miss Kenyon has its home and workshop, and links ten thousand years of human history.

In the Jordan Valley, some fifty miles north of Jericho, another town of great antiquity was named similarly after the Moon-God, Beth Yerah. It is set similarly by a fertile oasis in the

The New Old Land of Israel

rift. Its ruins stretch for nearly a mile along the south-western end of the sea of Galilee, where the river Jordan flows out of the lake and falls rapidly. It is also at a vital cross-road of the highways from north to south and west to east. Unlike Jericho, however, it is not mentioned in the Bible. Its history is pre-biblical and post-biblical. Yet in those periods it was a place of great importance, larger than Jericho. Professor Albright, the American archaeologist of the Bible land, judges that it may have been the capital city of North Canaan before Hazor. Its pottery of the early Bronze Age (2500 B.C.) has an attractive design and decoration, and resembles that of Anatolia. That suggests again Hittite influence. The oldest wall of the town was made of clay and straw bricks, and dates back to 3500 B.C. Above is a basalt wall, built of the local volcanic stone. Large parts, including a gate with orthostat slabs, are splendidly preserved, because the material is indestructible. Scholars have proved from the pottery fragments that the city was destroyed about 2300 B.C., that is, nearly a thousand years before the Hebrews entered the Promised Land.

The later period, of which the relics naturally are more plentiful, was the Hellenistic era, from 300 B.C., when Palestine was under the rule of the Ptolemies of Egypt. The place received from them a new name, Philoteria, in honour of the sister of Ptolemy Philadelphus, who gave his own name—Philadelphia—to the Biblical Ammon—now Amman again, the capital city of Jordan.

It was a big city for that time; the circuit of the fortified wall is a full mile. Between 2300 B.C. and 300 B.C. occupation of the site seems to have been interrupted more completely than at Jericho after the destruction of the Canaanite city by Joshua. In the ruins of the Hellenistic town precious jewellery and women's trinkets were discovered, pendants, decorated shells, a tube for perfume, a container for cosmetics, an instrument for colouring the eyebrows. They prove that women's tastes are constant through the ages. The chief monument of the later town is a Christian basilica, built over the ruins of a

Jericho and Beth Yerah

synagogue.

The site, with its antiquities of two eras covering three thousand years, is now attached to a cultural institute of Israel's Labour Federation, the Histadruth. Built as a tribute to a Labour leader who loved the place, and named Ohalo, meaning his tent, the institute is a centre of adult education and agricultural and technical conferences. This corner of Israel has a special appeal to the Labour Federation, which includes within its social services most of the co-operative and collective agricultural villages. For here was the earliest collective agricultural settlement or Kibbutz. Planted by a small group of idealist workers from Russia in the early years of the century, and called Dagania, the Place of Corn, it was first regarded as a fantastic experiment. But it endured and prospered. Today some two hundred collective villages are its offspring, distributed in all parts of the country. The prophet of the collective movement was a Russian-Jewish intellectual, a writer turned peasant, Abraham Gordon, who preached the gospel of manual work and of salvation by tilling the soil.

Inspired by Tolstoy, Gordon inculcated much the same way of life as was led two thousand years earlier in the land by the Essene sect whose Rules were found in the Dead Sea caves (see p. 149). Josephus described their community: 'Every man's possessions are intermingled with everybody else's, and there is one patrimony for all the brotherhood'. That also was the way of life of the earliest Christians: 'They that believed were together and had all things common'. The members of the Kibbutz cherish the same principles and are comrades one of another. There again the Biblical and the most recent ways of life are fused.

X

The Dead Sea: Caves, Scrolls and Citadels

A FEW miles south of Jericho the muddy Jordan runs into the heavy mineral-laden waters of the Dead Sea at the lowest place on the earth's surface, thirteen hundred feet below the level of the Mediterranean. The shores of the Sea are utterly desolate, bare of trees and vegetation. The precipitous, dry gorge of the Kidron, which starts below the walls of the city of Jerusalem, here makes its way to the sea under another name, meaning the Gorge of Fire. A few miles further south a limestone cliff rises steeply, some hundred feet from the shore. It is honeycombed with caves which have become famous in recent years. For they concealed fabulous buried libraries, with Hebrew manuscripts written probably two thousand years ago, before the Christian era, and at the latest, 1900 years ago. The amazing finds of antiquities have excited not only the learned world, but the man in the street. The first hoard of manuscripts, now known as the Dead Sea Scrolls, seven in number,* were found by two Bedu shepherds who were chasing their goats. As King Saul in the Bible story chased his asses and found a kingdom, so these Bedu, throwing stones at the goats, found a treasure of history. A goat suddenly disappeared; the shepherds followed, and espied a hole in the rock through which they peered into a chamber full of tall pottery jars. The jars contained leather

---

* There were indeed eleven scrolls, forming seven books. Those acquired by Professor Sukenik made up three books.

The Dead Sea: Caves, Scrolls and Citadels

scrolls tightly sealed with bitumen wrapping. The Bedu, looking for treasure of gold and silver, broke some, and damaged their contents. But others they brought out intact. That was in 1947, the year of destiny for Palestine and the State of Israel.

The Bedu took their strange loot to a cobbler-dealer in antiquities at Bethlehem, and sold them—for a song, as leather. The merchant hawked the scrolls, and through an Armenian agent offered some of them to Professor Sukenik, the archaeologist of the Hebrew University of Jerusalem. He recognised that the Hebrew letters, which were visible on a fragment of leather—all that he was allowed to examine—were exactly of the pattern on inscriptions of ossuaries (i.e. burial urns for bones) of the pre-Christian era, which he himself had discovered and deciphered. Convinced that the scrolls were important documents, he acquired three* for the University. The purchase was clinched on the day, November 29th, 1947, when the United Nations Assembly made their decision at Lake Success in favour of the creation of the Jewish State (Israel). On the next day grave troubles broke out between Jews and Arabs, and communication with Bethlehem was cut. The other four manuscripts were acquired by the Syrian Bishop of Bethlehem, and later were taken to America for sale. The Bishop failed to dispose of them, and in 1955 they were resold in America, in extraordinary conditions, to the son of Professor Sukenik, General Yadin, who was an archaeologist, working on the original three, but had been the Chief of Staff of the Army of Israel in the War of Independence. They were brought to Israel to be a national treasure, and deposited in a strong-room of the University of Jerusalem. A worthy 'shrine of the Book' is to be built for them in the University and National Library, and they will be a permanent possession of the People of the Book. They are for Israel a symbol of mystic continuity, linking the new State with the old and with the second Temple.

Of the seven original scrolls one is a complete, and one an in-

* See page 140

The New Old Land of Israel

complete, codex of the Book of Isaiah. Five are original works hitherto unknown to the Synagogue and the Church. All are judged to date from the period of the second Temple. They include a Book of Twenty Psalms or Hymns of Thanksgiving, each beginning with the words: "I give thanks to Thee, O Lord"; a commentary on the Book of the minor prophet, Habakkuk, an apocalyptic book describing the battle of the Forces of Light against the Forces of Darkness; a second apocryphal book, written not in Hebrew but in Aramaic, around the Bible stories of Noah, Abraham and Joseph in Genesis; and lastly, a *Manual of Discipline* of a sect which led a religious, ascetic life, were devoted to the study of the Law, and awaited the coming of the Messiah. The sect, whose way of life is set out in detail in the Book of Discipline, or Rule of the Community, is believed to be responsible for the buried libraries.

All the evidence points to it that the sect dwelt, during the troubled times of the Hundred Years Struggle with Rome, in this isolated retreat by the Dead Sea. There, as we know, both from Roman and Jewish historians, the monastic Essenes had their homes. The judgment of most scholars is that this sect was a branch of the Essenes, and that, when they felt that the day of doom was near, they buried their Holy Books, including the Bible scrolls, in the caves, so that they should not fall into the hands of the Romans. The scrolls were placed in stone jars, of which some have been preserved intact. Back in the days of the Prophet Jeremiah it was the practice to store Holy Scrolls in jars, 'so that they may continue many days'. (Jer. 32. 14). And the dry air of the Dead Sea region preserved them.

The romance of the discovery has been told by scholars like Professor Burrows and Dr. Yadin, and by brilliant writers like Edmund Wilson. It has become a popular tale, rivalling the detective stories of Sherlock Holmes. It is an amazing coincidence that the two-thousand-year-old picture of the struggle between the Jews and their enemies, the Kittim (identified generally with the Romans), should have been found in the very year when the Jews were girding themselves to fight for

The Dead Sea: Caves, Scrolls and Citadels

their independence and the restoration of their State. It is appropriate, too, that the transliteration and interpretation of the record should have been executed by one who had been Commander-in-Chief of the Forces of Israel in the contemporary struggle. It is not less amazing that the Hebrew script of many of the manuscripts is exactly like that in use in our own day in the Synagogue, where the books of the Mosaic Law are still read from manuscript leather scrolls.

The discovery did not end with the scrolls in the caves by the Sea. The Bedu Arabs, encouraged by their fortune, set about hunting for more treasure in caves. Indeed, it became the chief occupation of one of the tribes to chase manuscripts. The almost inaccessible caves, which lined the desert region between the Holy City of Bethlehem on the borders of the Judean Wilderness and the Dead Sea, proved to be a rich quarry. Manuscripts, Hebrew, Aramaic and Greek, of Books of the Bible and the Apocrypha, mostly in fragments, were gathered by the hundred. Moreover, Jewish ritual articles, the phylacteries, or leather strips which the Jews bind on the head and arm in prayer, and Mezuzot, scrolls of Bible verses fixed in a casket to the doorpost, and similar things were dug up. It was a trouble that the Bedu, who had no understanding of this new form of wealth, often ruined it before it came to the hands of scholars. They were disconcerting fellow-workers, and more nimble than the scientific experts. Orderly and scientific exploration of the caves was undertaken by the Antiquities Department of the Kingdom of Jordan, directed by a British scholar, and by the French Dominican Fathers of Jerusalem. Most of the treasure area was in that kingdom, though it extends to the oasis of Engedi, which is within the borders of Israel; and a few things have been found in that neighbourhood. Jewish scholars perversely were debarred from a part in the main search for what is of supreme interest to Jews. The barriers of the hot and cold war with the Arabs were impenetrable.

The English director of Antiquities in Jordan, Mr Harding, working with the French Dominican Father, Pére De Vaux,

The New Old Land of Israel

found the source, or one of the main sources, of the buried treasure. He was led to explore thoroughly a mound, a mile from the Caves, which had long been marked as a buried site of ancient habitation. It bore the Arabic name, Khirbet (meaning the ruin of) Qumran, and it should have attracted attention long since, because several medieval chroniclers, as well as archaeologists of the nineteenth century, had noted it. Here he found straightway a Jewish monastery of antiquity with rooms for a thousand communal, and a cultivable area by a spring. It included the relics of a synagogue, a ritual bath, the forerunner of the Christian baptistery, and a cemetery with over one thousand graves—but without inscriptions. The ritual bath was fed by an aqueduct half a kilometre in length. In the monastery were a store-room with hundreds of pottery bowls and beakers intact, and the ruins of a scriptorium, a room where the scrolls and manuscripts of the Order were written. The inkpots with the ink were still in their place, and in the debris was a pottery sherd, on which somebody had written the letters of the Hebrew alphabet in the form used in the manuscripts. Some apprentice scribe of the sect must have been trying out his hand before beginning his task.

Around the settlement of Qumran, pottery jars and sherds, similar in design to the pottery and jars in the Caves of the Scrolls, were strewn in abundance. Here, too, the archaeologists found Jewish and Roman coins dating over a period of 250 years, from about 100 B.C., when the Maccabean kings were rulers of the Land, to the middle of the 2nd century A.D. (136—140). The latter date is the period of the second Jewish war of Liberation from the Roman yoke. Subsequently, near the caves where the original scrolls were found, a searcher lighted on another cache of three hundred silver coins. Most were Roman, of the first and second centuries; the rest were Nabatean, from the Arab kingdom which was conquered by the Romans at the beginning of the second century. There were coins of the Roman Tenth Legion, such as had been found in Caesarea; and Josephus has recorded that this Legion was

The Dead Sea: Caves, Scrolls and Citadels

brought from Caesarea to the Dead Sea in the year 68. The range of the coins covers the Jewish struggle against Rome, ending with the desperate war of Simon Ben Koseba—renamed Bar Cochba, meaning Son of a Star (132—136).

For three years the Jews regained Jerusalem and a large part of the Land of Israel; and some of the coins bear a legend of the liberation. The revolt was crushed by Hadrian, the Roman emperor who drove back the Picts and Scots in Britain, and built the wall in Northern England to contain them. He had to recall the legions from Britain to fight the Jews. Among the documents found in the caves were copies of a proclamation of Bar Cochba, signed with his own hand and in his proper name, calling the Jews to arms and giving orders to his lieutenants. In the same spot they found an inkpot with dry ink of lead-black and gum. It might have been used by Bar Cochba for writing the proclamation; and there were reports addressed to him, 'the Prince of Israel'. Here in this Jewish Monte Cassino were the secret headquarters of the rebellion.

We learn from Josephus, the Jewish historian of the first century, and from Pliny, the famous Roman man of letters of the same generation, that the monastic Essenes had their principal retreat in the region. They were mystics, devoted students of the Bible and the Apocrypha, and part of their ritual was the bath of purification. And they shared everything in common. Josephus wrote of them in *The Wars of the Jews* (Book 2, Chapter 8): 'These men despise riches . . . Nor is there anyone to be found among them who have more than another. For it is their law that those who come to them must let what they have be common to the whole order . . . Nor do they buy or sell anything to one another; but everyone gives what he hath to him that wanteth it, and receives from it again in return what may be convenient for him . . . They believe that the principle of brotherhood is the natural relationship of men. They eat their meals in prayerful silence as if it were a holy ritual . . .

'Their piety towards God is very extraordinary. Before sun-

The New Old Land of Israel

rise they speak not a word about profane matters, but recite certain prayers, which they have received from their forefathers, as if making supplication for its rising . . . If anyone hath a mind to come over to the sect, he is not immediately admitted, but is prescribed the method of living which they use for a year, while he continues excluded . . . They are among those who undertake to foretell things to come by reading the holy books and using various sorts of purification, and being perpetually conversant in the teaching of the prophets.'

Philo, the Jewish philosopher of Alexandria, writing about them a little earlier than Josephus, in a treatise 'Every Good Man is Free', explains their name Essenes: 'It is, I think, a variation of the Greek word for holiness, because they have shown themselves specially devout in the service of God, not by offering sacrifices of animals but by resolving to sanctify their minds. They live in villages and avoid the cities, because of the iniquities which have become inveterate among city dwellers. They are almost alone in all mankind in that they have no money and no land, by their deliberate choice . . . They have a single treasure and disburse everything in common: their clothes are held in common, and they take their food through public meals.'

The Roman Pliny in his *Natural History* describes them more briefly; and probably is repeating what he had been told: 'On the west-side of the Dead Sea, out of range of the noxious exhalations of the coast, is the solitary tribe of the Essenes. It is remarkable beyond all other tribes in the world, as it has no women and no money, and only palm trees for company. Day by day the tribe is recruiting by numerous accessions of persons tired of life, and driven thither by the waves of fortune to adopt their manners.'

An eminent scholar, Professor Dupont-Sommer, has made an ingenious suggestion that the name Essenes, which has hitherto not received a certain derivation, may be a Greek corruption of the Hebrew '*etza*', meaning Council, that occurs constantly in the documents. The sect in the Manual is known

The Dead Sea: Caves, Scrolls and Citadels

variously as the Community of the Covenant, the Alliance, and the Council. The priests of the Order are known as the Sons of Zadok; and the name Essenes, which is found only in Josephus, Philo and Pliny, may have been a slang term. Of their doctrines and way of life we know more now through those documents than ever Josephus and Philo of Alexandria knew, or, at least, recorded.

In the first years after the discovery, most scholars were agreed that the scrolls and the fragments belonged to a library of the Essenes. But another theory was put forward in 1957 by Professor Driver of Oxford and Dr Cecil Roth, the Jewish historian. They ascribed the books, and particularly the Manual of Discipline, to the sect of Zealots, fanatical Jewish patriots, who in the first century fought out desperate resistance against the Romans. Historically attractive, the identification of the dedicated religious Order with the political extremists and terrorists is paradoxical, and a little difficult to sustain. The description in the Manual is of a body retired from the world and engaged in religious exercises. It is a possible synthesis of the two theories that the settlement in this region of caves and natural hideouts, which is also not far from the region of the cave of Adullam—King David's retreat (I Sam. 22.1)—included both religious votaries and others who combined the martial spirit with piety. Those qualities went hand in hand, as they did in the period of Oliver Cromwell and the Levellers.

Other caves which have been explored in the neighbourhood have yielded more copies of the Manual, of the Book of the Battle of the Forces of Light, and of the Thanksgiving hymns. They go to support the idea that the original settlement at Qumran overflowed in the emergency times. It is possible, then, that Zealot warriors were mingled with other-worldly saints; and they may have written some of the books, particularly the Battle Scrolls.

The mass of manuscripts, diverse as they are in content and form, are linked together by a common devotion to the text of the Bible on the one hand, and to Messianic hopes on the other.

The New Old Land of Israel

In the first place come the copies of all the books of the Hebrew Bible, except only the Book of Esther, which may not have been accepted into the Canon of the sect because of the favour it shows to foreign rule, by the Persians. Apart from the two codices of Isaiah, the books are in fragments, but even so the bits and pieces throw important light on the text. Some fragments are in the early Hebrew script, and may date even from the third century B.C. Then the commentaries on the Bible books, e.g. of the minor prophets, Micah, Habakkuk and Nahum, as well as on the books of Moses and the major prophets. They contain an inner mystical interpretation verse by verse, similar to the Allegories of Philo, the Jewish philosopher of Alexandria, which were composed in Greek about the same period. The commentary on Genesis, one of the seven original scrolls, however, is different. It is in Aramaic, and is the oldest known manuscript in that language, which was the common speech in the time of Christ. Such parts of it as have been deciphered are an embroidered popular story of the life of Noah and Abraham, and give an account of Abraham's journeys through the Bible land, which is a precious source of ancient geography. We have now the Hebrew text of several apocryphal and apocalyptic books hitherto known only in Greek, and of several that were not known at all. One is the *Prayer of Nabonides*, who was the last King of Babylon, and is represented as a dreamer of apocalyptic dreams.

Next there are the scrolls of the Battle, the Hymns, and the Manual. The three are closely connected. For the sectaries, whose rule is set out in the Manual and accessory documents, are the Sons of Light—the Covenanters—who at the end of days are to do battle against the pagan Sons of Darkness and their allies among the aristocratic Jews, 'the violators of the covenant'. The scrolls in several copies tell of their triumph, and give the detail of their order of battle and of the prayers which they recite before and during combat. The Hymns of Thanksgiving, also in several copies, may be the Songs of Triumph. The angelic hosts are involved as well as the human.

The Dead Sea: Caves, Scrolls and Citadels

For the sectaries believed in a source of evil, Belial or Satan, whose cohorts engage the good angels and are finally worsted.

The Book of Discipline centres around the 'teacher of Justice' or righteousness, who was done to death by a wicked high priest, but will be resurrected and lead his people to victory. His followers went into exile to Damascus—which may be a real or symbolic place. The commentaries on the minor prophets refer to that exile, and to the wicked priest, 'the Man of Lies'. They refer also to the instrument of vengeance, 'the chief of the Kings of Javan'. Some scholars identify the wicked priest with the Maccabee priest-King Hyrcanus II, who in the first half of the last century B.C. persecuted the pious Pharisees; and the instrument of vengeance with the Roman Pompey, who captured Jerusalem in 63 B.C., and took prisoner the Maccabee prince.

We have by extraordinary fortune other ancient Hebrew documents bearing on a sect of Covenanters who went to Damascus. Just fifty years before the discovery of the Dead Sea Scrolls, an eminent Jewish scholar, Solomon Schechter, discovered a treasure of ancient and medieval manuscripts in the buried archives—Geniza it was called—of the most ancient synagogue of Cairo. The hoard was still bigger and more varied than that of the scrolls and fragments of the Dead Sea caves and Qumran. The writings were nearly a thousand years later in date, but there was a large fragment of a document describing the way of life of a Damascus sect of the early centuries, which corresponds exactly with fragments found in the caves. The similarities of the doctrines with those of the Manual of Discipline are too great to be a coincidence. The documents of Qumran and the Cairo manuscripts together seem to prove that the sect left a permanent mark on Jewish thought, which survived its activity as a sect.

One of the most important and controversial aspects of the scrolls is the light they shed on the genesis of Christianity and the spiritual climate of the times. What seems to emerge is that much of the content of early Christian thought and practice,

The New Old Land of Israel

hitherto believed to be derived from Hellenistic influence, has its source in the life and beliefs of this—Essene?—sect, if it is that. The faith in the Teacher of Justice, the ideals of celibacy and community of property, the common meal, the Messianic interpretation of Scripture, the idea of the Messiah begotten by God, and a second Messiah of the royal line of David, are parallel with the beliefs of the early Christian congregations. The Jewish Sectaries sought God in the same desert region where John the Baptist preached. It is not impossible that John was a member of the Qumran community. There is, indeed, one striking difference, that the Jewish votaries of the Teacher of Righteousness were inspired by the vision and conviction of the triumph of Jews over Romans and of Judaism over the pagan creeds, and were prepared to battle for their faith. The Kingdom of God on earth, they believed, was at hand.

One of the scrolls found in the caves near Qumran resisted unravelling for five years. It was not of leather like the rest, but of copper, and it required the nicest scientific skill to open it without destroying the contents. That was achieved finally by a chemist of Manchester University, and the scroll was revealed. It was written, not in classical Hebrew, but in the popular language of mixed Hebrew and Aramaic, which was also the language of the Mishna, the Oral Law compiled in the second century. The plaque had been hurriedly rolled, and the lettering showed signs of haste. It turned out to be a catalogue of treasure of gold and silver, and of the places where it was buried. The places extend over a hundred miles north and south of Jerusalem, from Shekem (Nablus) in the centre of Palestine, to Hebron on the borders of the Negev. The treasure of talents and shekels, if it really existed, must be that of the Temple of Jerusalem. Whether it was retrieved and buried before the final destruction there is nothing to show. So far the treasure-hunters of our day, following the clues of the scroll, have had no luck. Perhaps some digger will yet light on the El Dorado of Antiquity. We may hope that it will not be a predatory Bedu.

It is the contention of Professor Driver and Dr Roth that the

The Dead Sea: Caves, Scrolls and Citadels

'teacher of justice' was a Zealot priestly leader, Menahem, referred to in the history of the Jewish Wars by Josephus. He led a revolutionary movement against the Romans in 66 A.D. and was killed. It is suggested that a group of his devoted and fanatical followers, who retired from Jerusalem to the Dead Sea region, made a desperate stand against the Romans at Massada, and composed the commentaries and the Manual of Discipline between 66 and 73. In the latter year, we shall see, they perished by their own hands, having previously buried their library. They were associated with the Alliance or the Covenanters, who are the subject of the document found in the Cairo Geniza, and who returned from Damascus and found a home in Qumran. Together—so the theory goes—they formed a kind of republic of intransigent millenarians. The Lion of Wrath, referred to in some of the documents, is identified with the Jewish Warrior John of Gischala, who was captured by the Romans and led in chains in the triumph of Titus. Finally, it is suggested that the author of the copper scroll about the buried treasure was another Zealot Priest, who had control of the Temple, and recorded the Temple gold and silver wealth which was hidden, and should be recovered after the victory was won. The copper document, at any rate, may be ascribed to the Zealots. It therefore supports to some extent the theory that among the inhabitants in the Qumran Monastery were religious Zealots, and that part of the literature among the scrolls was written by them.

Jewish and Christian scholars are only at the beginning of the examination of the vast literary treasure. After a period of scepticism by a few about the date of the manuscripts and fragments, and suggestions of medieval forgeries, their genuineness is almost universally admitted. The evidence of the writing, of the contents of the books, of the jars and the linen wrapping, lastly, of the ink which has been tested by physicists and chemists, all point to a period before the Christian era. A new scientific way of fixing, not the date but, the era of antique sites and relics is the application of the wonders of chemistry.

The New Old Land of Israel

By radio-carbon tests of any organic matter which is found on the site, the age can be told within a range of 100-200 years. That test has been used for the linen wrappings of some scrolls; and limits the range of their age to the period between 100 B.C. and 100 A.D. It decisively rules out the possibility of a medieval origin. So suddenly, and incredibly, we have an abundance of Hebrew manuscripts older by nearly 1000 years than the earliest hitherto known. Before the scrolls and the library of Qumran were unearthed, the earliest Bible manuscripts were tiny fragments of the Greek scripture found among Egyptian papyri of the first and second century B.C. The newly found source is a link between the records in the Bible and Apocrypha and the manuscripts which were produced in the Christian monasteries. It enormously increases our knowledge of Jewish thought in a critical period of religious history, and our knowledge of the ideals, rites and doctrines of a Jewish sect in the age when the Christian community came into being. To Israel the discovery of the scrolls seems a symbol of mystic continuity which links the State with the destruction of the second Temple.

A few miles south of the caves and Qumran is Engedi, meaning the Spring of the Kid. It is a place famous in the Bible and post-Biblical literature for its fertility in the midst of utter desolation. Pliny, in his account of the Essenes, also refers to that character. 'Second only to Jerusalem in the fertility of its land and its palm groves, but now, like Jerusalem, a heap of ashes.' The one place on the western shore of the Dead Sea which has abundant fresh water, it is today a frontier-post of Israeli settlers, a collective group of young pioneers. They came in 1951, and have reclaimed the land which, in the Mandate days, was occupied by a few Bedu Arabs. It is physically the lowest agricultural village in Israel. They have made a fertile oasis of fruit plantations and vegetable gardens. Engedi's history goes back to King David, who found refuge there from the wrath of Saul, and to King Solomon, who in the Song of Songs compared his beloved with 'A cluster of camphire in the

The Dead Sea: Caves, Scrolls and Citadels

vineyards of Engedi'. Archaeologists exploring it in the recent years have found an unexpected harvest of antiquity, evidence of continual settlement throughout the first kingdom of Judah, 1000—600 B.C. A network of terraces, walls and canals proves how the water was carried from the spring. They found, too, pottery and glass from the period of the second Commonwealth, of the Maccabees, to the Great Revolt against the Romans. Here was another centre of guerilla resistance.

Moreover, at Engedi as at Beersheba, they have found habitations of prehistoric man dug in the soft side of the hills, and approached by shafts and galleries. For the sake of security the dwellings were invisible from the outside, and they have remained intact to the present day. They contain remarkable works of art. For man thus early cherished some sense of beauty, and made vases gracefully shaped and decorated with patterns painted in red. Their bracelets, necklaces and other ornaments prove the existence of an original craftsmanship. Small ivory figures, in which they represent themselves adoring some divinity, witness to their sense of religion, and also to their sense of form.

In the wilderness adjoining Engedi, within the territory of Israel, the searchers found traces of a Roman camp and caves filled with skeletons, pottery vessels, bowls and baskets. In the debris there was one inscribed potsherd with Hebrew letters, proving that Jews had occupied them. A father of the early Christian Church tells that the Jewish rebels, after the defeat of Bar Cochba (135 A.D.), refused to surrender, and fortifying themselves in caves, were besieged and starved to death. Most of the skeletons in the caves were of women and children, which suggests that the men broke out in a sortie and were killed.

Opposite Engedi, on the eastern side of the Dead Sea, rises the hill of Machaerus, some four thousand feet above the Sea. Here was a fortress, built by Herod the Great as another retreat, and later the residence of Herod Antipas. Here John the Baptist was imprisoned in the dungeon of the palace, and here he was

The New Old Land of Israel

murdered to please Salome.

Some ten miles south of Engedi a rocky hill rises four hundred metres sheer above the surrounding desert and the Dead Sea. From ancient times till today it has kept the Hebrew name Masada, which means Fortress. On the summit a level heart-shaped area, about seven hundred metres long, is the fortified citadel. Deep precipices cut off the rock on all sides, and the summit is accessible only by two narrow snake-paths. Masada deserves its name. It is a fortress of Nature, and was the scene of the last desperate stand of the Jews against the Romans in the Seven Years War, 66—73 A.D., which brought the State to an end. Three years after the destruction of the Temple of Jerusalem by Titus, a heroic band of the Zealots, 960 men, women and children, held out there against the Roman Legions. The siege operations were carried out with a Roman thoroughness, which is visible. Eight camps were erected at the base of the fortress, and a rampart with towers surrounded them. The Roman Legions threw up a ramp—which is still visible—on one side, and placed their siege engines and battering rams to breach the wall. When the Jewish defenders saw that the fort was about to fall, they chose death rather than captivity and killed each other. The last to live set fire to the buildings.

Josephus, who had been commander of the Jewish forces in Galilee in the first years of the revolt, but had surrendered long before to the Romans, and had an uneasy conscience, puts into the mouth of the Zealots' leader a moving speech. It is on the theme that it was better to die by their own hands than to fall into the hands of the Romans. Josephus must have conjured the speech from his own remorseful reflections. And he tells how the Romans entering the fortress, and encountering the mass of the slain, admired the nobility of the resolve and the contempt for death which the Jews displayed (B.J. VII 92).

Our knowledge of the history of Masada is derived almost entirely from the works of Josephus, the Antiquities of the Jews, and the Jewish Wars against the Romans. Two Roman

The Dead Sea: Caves, Scrolls and Citadels

authors of the first century, Strabo and Pliny, make a casual mention of the rock and the pitch issuing from its crevices; and that is all. Josephus tells that the fortress was built by Jonathan, the brother of Judas the Maccabee, in the middle of the second century B.C., as a place of refuge from the Hellenistic armies. It was vastly expanded and reconstructed by Herod the Great a hundred years later. In the year 40 B.C. Herod fled there with his mother, his younger brother and sister, and his betrothed Mariamne, after Jerusalem had fallen into the hands of the Parthians who had made his rival, of the Maccabean House, Matathias Antigonus, king. He placed a garrison of 800 men to protect the women, and stored supplies of grain and water and other necessities. Antigonus blockaded the garrison, which suffered from lack of water till providential rain one night filled the cisterns. Herod raised the siege, and later rebuilt the fortress and furnished it as a refuge for himself, 'suspecting a two-fold danger, peril on the one hand from the Jewish people lest they should depose him and restore their former dynasty to power; and the more serious danger from Cleopatra, Queen of Egypt'.

Herod enclosed the summit by a double casemate wall built of white stone, six metres high and four metres wide. The wall had 37 towers, each 25 metres high. The interior of the fortress was used for cultivation; but he built great storehouses and supplied them with quantities of wheat sufficient for years, wine and oil, all kinds of pulses and quantities of dates. He built himself also a palace below the walls towards the northern slope of the rock. To assure the water he ordered the cutting of cisterns in the rock at each spot of habitation, both on the summit and about the palace, and procured a supply 'as ample as where springs are available'.

After Herod's death and the deposition of his son by the Romans, Masada was occupied by a Roman garrison, A.D. 61-66. It was during that time presumably that Josephus, who lived with the Essene sectarians near the Dead Sea, visited it, and acquired his accurate knowledge of the stupendous structure.

The New Old Land of Israel

In the first days of the Jewish Revolt (66 A.D.) a group of Zealots under Menahem, the son of Judah the Galilean (see page 151) attacked the fort, captured it, put the Roman garrison to the sword, and replaced it by a garrison of their own. They remained in possession through the seven years of the war, 66—73. They made their headquarters—and their death chamber—in Herod's palace. Sir George Adam Smith, the author of the classical Historical Geography of the Holy Land, written seventy years ago, has said about them: 'The fire, which had scorched Israel's borders for a thousand years, burst into a still more fatal flame within her. The splendid suicide of Israel, begun in Galilee, was consummated on the rocks of Masada, half way between Jerusalem and the Mount of Esau.'

The first modern exploration of the mountain was made by Jewish Youth groups led by an amateur archaeologist, a member of a collective settlement, who had come to Israel from Glasgow, before the State of Israel. A few Gentile scholars exploring the hill had noted part of the Herodian structures as described by Josephus, but they had not been able to reach it.

In the last years Israel archaeologists, led by Professor Mazar of the Hebrew University, have begun a thorough exploration of the mountain, and revealed history almost as sensational as that unearthed in the monastery of Qumran. On the uppermost platform overhanging the precipice they uncovered a striking Hellenistic building; the interior was adorned with columns and Corinthian capitals. In front of it a semi-circular terrace, from which steps led to the lower level. They found a secret stairway, cut in the rock and invisible from the outside, penetrating to the lowest platform. Here were vaulted sub-structures, the heart of the palace, with a hall surrounded by a colonnade four metres high. The palace was a remarkable piece of engineering, built on the desolate cliff-top like an eagle's eyrie, overlooking the desert of Judea and the Dead Sea. But much of the construction was shoddy, stone and plaster painted to resemble marble.

A later expedition of the archaeologists in 1956 found an Aramaic and a Hebrew inscription. The latter ended with the

The Dead Sea: Caves, Scrolls and Citadels

words: Hanan Ben Shinar from Shammar, (the name of a place). It was written in black ink, and the writing was similar to the square script of the Dead Sea Scrolls. May this be the record of the name of one of the Zealot defenders? Perhaps they cast lots for the order of suicide, and his lot survived the conflagration which destroyed the rest. The later expedition, moreover, found at the base of the mountain a stupendous series of cisterns, which would hold altogether eight million gallons. They were fed by an aqueduct from a dry river-bed to the north which, like others in the desert region, becomes a roaring torrent for a day or days of the winter rain. The aqueduct brought the water to holes of the rock, which before were thought to be the cells of Anchorites. The discovery confirms the story of Josephus that Herod cut in the rock numerous large tanks as reservoirs for the water. The expedition found that a path led from the cisterns at lower level to another on a summit with a capacity of eight hundred thousand gallons. They found, too, under the plaster in a room of the palace, drawings of two ships, which point to the maritime interests of the Herods and the Jews.

The southern end of the Dead Sea, a few miles from Masada, is marked by a hill or cliff of rock salt. That is Sodom; to the Arabs the Hill of Lot. Traditionally it is the pillar of salt to which Lot's wife was turned when she looked back in the flight from the wicked towns of Sodom and Gomorrah. Today there is a humming centre of industry and chemical plant.

Paradoxically the Dead Sea itself, which Professor George Adam-Smith described as 'this awful hollow, this hell with the sun shining on it', is being turned into an inexhaustible source of physical fertility by the exploitation of its wealth of potash and other salts. And the region round the Dead Sea, desolate and waste, is being turned to a parallel source of the history of Judaism and of early Christianity.

INDEX

Abbahu, Rabbi, 62
Abd-Khiba, 33 f
Abda, ruins, 117
Abdul Malik, Caliph, 36
Abraham, patriarch, 115, 133
Absalom, tomb, 42
Accadian, language, 23 f
Acre, 40, 90
Agrippa, king, 42
Ahab, king, 20, 95
Aila, see Elath
Ain Duk, 136
Ain Harod, 99
Akaba, gulf, 116 f, 124 ff
Akhenaton, 33
Akiva, rabbi, 62
Alexander The Great, 39
Alexandria, 40
Allenby, Lord, 94, 119
Alphabets, 24 f
Amarna, Tel, 33, 68
Amenophis, Pharaoh, 107
Amman, 40, 138
Amos, prophet, 20
Antioch, 40
Antony, Mark, 25
Arab, conquest, 45
Aramaic, language and script, 25
Armageddon, 94
Arraba, gorge, 123, 127
Ashdod, 87
Askalon, 85 ff
Assyrian, language, 16
  script, 26
Athlit, 91
Auja, town in Sinai, 117

Baal, god, 26, 108
Babylon, empire, 38
Baibars, sultan, 59, 63, 86
Baisan, see Beth Shaan
Baldwin II, king, 86
Balfour, forest, 110
Bar Kochba, 110
Bar Saba, tomb, 43, 121
Bedu, Arabs, 140 ff
Beersheba, 115 ff
Ben Gurion, Prime Minister, 120 ff

Ben Shemen, school, 74
Beth Alpha, 98
Beth Horon, 56
Beth Shaan, 27, 40, 89 ff, 95 ff
Beth Shearim, 109 ff
Beth Yerah, 137 ff
Byblos, Phoenician town, 70, 83
Byzantine, monastery, 30

Caesarea, history, 61 ff
Canaanite, religion, 26
Carmel, caves, 21 ff
  ridge, 89
Christianity, early, 149
  religion of Roman Empire, 43 ff
Cleopatra, queen, 135, 155
Clermont-Ganneau, 37, 67, 70
Conder, Colonel, 17
Constantine, emperor, 44
Copper, use of, 26, 55, 115
Covenanters, sect, 149
Crusades, 46 f, 97, 118
Cuneiform, script, 23
Cyprus, 26
Cyrus, 38

Dagania, village, 139
Dagon, worship, 26, 87
Dahab, Gulf of Akaba, 127
Damascus, sect, 149
Daniel, Canaanite god, 26
David, king and Engedi, 152
  Jerusalem, 33 ff
  citadel of, 35
  tomb of, 36
Dead Sea, caves, 28, 140 ff
  scrolls, 28, 49, 140 ff
Deborah, prophetess, 92
Decapolis, 91, 102
De Vaux, Father, 143
Dimona, township, 123
Discipline, manual of, 142, 148 ff
Disraeli, quoted, 32
Diezengoff, mayor of Tel-Aviv, 60
Dor, town, 89 ff
Driver, professor, 150
Dura-Europos, synagogue, 99

Index

Edom, land of, 116
Egypt, civilisation, 24
  diplomatic documents, 33
  empire, 33
Ein Karim, 51
Elath, 121 ff
Elisha, prophet, 130
Emek, central valley, 89
En-Gedi, 152 ff
Esbeita, ruins, 117
Essenes, 145
Etzion-Geber, port, 55
Eusebius, Church-father, 63
Evenari, Professor, 116
Ezechiel, quoted, 27

Frederick II, emperor, 47

Galilee, 100 ff
Gamaliel, rabbi, 86, 112
Garrod, Professor D., 22
Garstang, Professor, 103 f
Gath, Philistine town, 84
Gaza, 85
Gedalia, 38, 82
Geniza, Cairo, 149
Gethsemane, garden, 43
Gezer, 19 ff
  excavations, 66 ff
  inscriptions, 25
Gihon, spring, 34
Gill, Eric, 49
Gilgamesh, epic poem, 94
Gluck, Professor N., 124
Goethe, quoted, 30
Gordon, A. 139

Habakkuk, commentary on, 142
Habiri, 24, 34
Hadassah, organisation, 72
Hadrian, emperor, 44
Haifa, harbour, 54
Haram, area of Jerusalem, 77
Harding, 143
Hardy, Thomas, 95
Hattin, battle, 46
Hawkes, Miss Jacquetta, 22
Hazor, 48, 50, 120 ff
Hebrew, script, 24 f, 37, 69, 80
  University, 48, 50, 120
Hedjaz, railway, 98, 125

Helena, empress, 44, 135
  and Askalon, 86
Herod, and Caesarea, 62 f
  and Jericho, 135
  grave, 42
  temple, 153
Herzl, tomb, 47, 57
Hezekiah, tunnel, 37
  pool of, 38
Hieroglyphs, inscriptions, 24
Hilkiah, seal, 82
Himyar, Jews of, 113
Hiram, king of Tyre, 54
Histadruth, 139
Hittite, civilisation, 27
  language, 23
Huleh, lake, 100
Hurrites, language, 26
Hurva, synagogue, 47
Hyksos, dynasty, 57, 93

Isaiah, codex, 142
Israel, people of archaeology, 29 ff

Jabin, king of Hazor, 101 f
Jaffa, history, 53 ff
  orange, 59
Jannaeus, Alexander, king, 58, 91
Jebusites, 33
Jehosaphat, vale of, 42
Jeremiah, prophet, 38, 79, 142
Jericho, excavation, 20, 28, 129 ff
Jerusalem, Chapter 2
  biblical, 32 ff
  Hellenistic, 40
  Herod's, 41 f
  Roman siege, 43 ff
  Christian, 44
  Moslem, 45
  Crusaders, 46
  modern, 47 ff
  Museum, 48
  in Israel State, 50 f
Jesus, 135
Jezebel, queen, 20
Jezreel, vale, 89, 95
Jochanan, Ben Zaccai, synagogue, 47
John the Baptist, 153
Jonathan, Maccabee, 86
Jordan, kingdom, 30
Josephus, historian, 39, 111, 139, 145 ff, 150 ff

Index

Joshua, invasion, 20, 33
Josiah, king, 92
Jotba, island, 127
Judah, rabbi, 111 ff
Judas Maccabaeus, 155
Judea, wilderness, 28
Judean Foothills, see Chapter 4
Julian, emperor, 45
Justinian, emperor, 87

Kassileh, Tel, 55
Kenyon, Dr K., 130 ff
Kibbutz, collective, 84, 111, 139
Kidron, valley, 34, 38
Kings, tombs of, 42
Kitchener, Lord, 17, 74
Kittim, (Romans), 142

Lachish, 25, 38, 77 ff
  letters of, 49, 78 ff
Latakia, 23
Lawrence, T. E., 117
Lod, (Lydda), 75
Lot, brother of Abraham, 123
Louis IX, king, 63

Maccabees, revolt, 40, 70, 73
Mac-Alister, Professor, 20, 67
Machaerus, fortress, 153
Madeba, map, 45
Mandeville, Sir John, 73
Mari, archives, 102
Masada, fortress, 154 ff
Mazar, Professor, 110, 156
Mefjir, palace, 136
Megiddo, 25, 89 ff, 92 ff, 107
Menahem, Zealot leader, 156
Merenptah, Pharaoh, 68
Merom, waters, 100, 102
Mesopotamia, civilisation, 23 f
Meshatta, 136
Messiah, belief, 150
Mikveh, Israel, school, 60
Mishna, oral law, 150
Modin or Modiin, 40, 72 ff
Mohammed, religion, 118
Montefiore, Sir Moses, 35, 48, 60
Moriah, Mount, 17, 32, 36
Moslem, worship, 45 f
Murray, Hall, Elath, 126
Mycenaean, Pottery, 104 f

Nabateans, 116 f, 121

Naharia, Canaanite shrine, 69
Napoleon, invasion of Egypt, 16, 59
Natufian, Culture, 131
Nebuchadnezzar, invasion, 38
Negev, exploration, 28, 115 ff
Nehemiah, 39, 118
Netofa, town, 39
Neuville, Consul, 22

Olives, Mount of, 40, 45, 113
Omar, Mosque of, 36, 46
Omayad, Caliphs, 136 f
Onkelos, at Askalon, 86
Ophel, Mount, 17, 32, 34
Ophir, Gold, 36, 56
Origen, Church-father, 63
Ossuaries, Jerusalem, 43

Palestine Exploration Fund, 16, 74, 130
Papyrus, use of, 82 f
Paul, St., 62
Pekah, king of Israel, 103, 105
Peter, St., at Jaffa, 59
Petra, 117
Petrie, Sir Flinders, 18
Philadelphia (Amman), 138
Philistines, 35, 54, 85
Philo of Alexandria, 148
Phoenician, language and script, 18 f
Pliny, 91, 145, 152, 155
Pompey, 41, 91
Pontius Pilate, 62
Pottery, importance of, 17 ff
Ptolemies, 40, 138

Qumran, monastery, 144 f

Ramases, dynasty, 35, 58, 85, 90
Ramat Rahel, Jerusalem, 39
  Gan, 61
Ramon, peak, 122
Rephaim, vale, 35
Richard I, king, 59
Robinson, Edward, 16
Rockefeller, John, 21, 93
  Museum, 49
Rosetta, Stone, 16
Roth, Dr C., 150
Rothschild, Edmond de, 64, 71, 91
  James de, 64
Rowe, A., excavations, 69

Index

Saladin, 46, 69
Samaria, excavated, 20
  frontier village, 30
Samuel, Lord, 48, 72
Sanhedrin, tombs of, 42
Sarona, village, 61
Saul, king, 96
Schechter, S., 149
Scopus, Mount, 48
Scythians, 96
Scythopolis, 96
Seleucid, empire, 40
Semitic Alphabet, 24 ff
Seneth, Hannah, 64
Sennacherib, 37, 77 f
Shishak, Pharaoh, 92
Siloam, pool, 34
Simon the Just, High Priest, 40
Simon Maccabee, 71
Sinai Campaign, 127
  Script, 69, 89
Smith, Sir George Adam, 19, 156 f
Sodom, Potash works, 123, 157
Solomon, King: Jerusalem, 35
  Song of, 152
  stables, 37, 93
Stanhope, Hester, 86
Stanley, Dean, 47
St. George, 76
Starkey, 78
Strabo, Roman writer, 135
Sukenik, Professor, 43, 140 ff
Suliman, sultan, 47
Sumerian, language, 23
Synagogues, ancient, 41

Taanach, 89, 92
Tabitha, of Jaffa, 59
Talmud, 111 f
Tantura, 95 f
Tel, nature of, 17 f
  Amarna, see Amarna
Tel-Aviv, 53 ff

Templars, knights, 46
Temple, of Jerusalem, 32 f
Tenth Legion, 43, 125
Thutmosis III, 92
Tiberias Sanhedrin, 112
Tiglath Pileser, king, 56
Timna, copper mines, 127
Tiran, island, 127 f
Titus, siege of Jerusalem, 43
Turks, Young, 119
Turville-Petre, 21

Ugarit, civilisation, 23 f
  religion, 36
  scripts, 25
UNESCO, station Beersheba, 120
Ur, of Chaldees, 115, 117, 130
Uzziah, king, 116, 124

Warren, Sir Charles, 17
Western Wall, of Temple, 36, 45
William II, emperor, 47
Wilson, Sir Charles, 17
  Edmund, 142
Woolley, Sir L., 117

Yadin, Dr Y. and Hazor, 101 ff
  Dead Sea Scrolls, 141 ff
Yahud, (Judea), 39
Yalud, battle, 97
Yarkon, river, 55/56
Yarmuk, battle, 97
Yeruham, tel, 122
Yerushalaim, 39

Zachariah, tomb of, 42
Zangwill, I., 74
Zealots, 151 ff
Zephaniah, prophet, 88
Zerubbabel, temple, 32, 38, 54
Zin, wilderness, 117
Zion, Mount, 17, 32 f
Zoar, town, 123 f